D0849388

Solfège, Ear Training, Rhythm, Dictation, and Music Theory

To my students, whose
interest in learning
inspired this book

Marta Árkossy Ghezzo

Solfège, Ear Training, Rhythm, Dictation, and Music Theory: A Comprehensive Course

The University of Alabama Press
University, Alabama

ACKNOWLEDGMENTS

I wish to express my deepest gratitude and appreciation to Diane N. Battung for her suggestions and enthusiastic cooperation in reviewing the text of the manuscript.

Special thanks to the following publishers for their consideration in granting permission to
use the examples included in the "Musical Examples for Further Reference": Alphonse Leduc
(Paris), Akadémiai Kiadó (Budapest), Belwin Mills Publishing Corp. (N.Y.), Boosey and
Hawkes Inc. (N.Y.), Breitkopf & Härtel (Wiesbaden), Aldo Bruzzichelli (Firenze), J. & W.
Chester/Edition Wilhelm Hansen London Ltd. (London), Ernst Eulenburg Ltd. (London), Carl Fisher, Inc.
(N.Y.), Harvard University Press (Cambridge), Heugel & Cie (Paris), Edwin F. Kalmus (N.Y.),
Lea Pocket Scores (N.Y.), M C A Music Inc. (N.Y.), McGraw-Hill Book Co. (N.Y.), Moeck Verlag
(Celle), Nagels-Verlag (Kassel), C. F. Peters Corp. (N.Y.), Prentice-Hall, Inc. (Englewood Cliffs),
Polskie Wydawnictwo Muzyczne (Krakow), G. Ricordi & Co. s.p.a. (Milano), G. Schirmer, Inc.
(N.Y.), The John Day Company, Inc. (N.Y.), Universal-Edition A. G. Wien, Seesaw Music Corp.
(N.Y.), Editura Didactică si Pedagogică (Bucuresti), Editura Muzicală a Uniunii Compositorilor
din R.S.R., Associated Music Publishers (N.Y.), Universal Edition (London), Universal Edition
(Leipzig), Mills Music, Inc. (N.Y.), Broude Bros., Leeds Music Corp., Elkan-Vogel, Inc., Universal
Edition A.G. (Wien), Theodor Presser Company, Pennsylvania).

Library of Congress Cataloging in Publication Data

Ghezzo, Marta Árkossy
   Music theory, ear training, rhythm, solfège,
and dictation, a comprehensive course.

   Bibliography: p.
   1. Music—Instruction and study. I. Title.
MT6.G477M9   780   78-16047
ISBN 0-8173-6403-X

Contents

Preface

Enabling skills enable a musician to be a musician. They are the fundamental ear, eye, and mind proficiencies, that converging point where singers, instrumentalists, conductors, composers, and theoreticians all must encounter one and the same set of things-to-be-mastered-first-of-all.

It may be that in principle virtually everyone can acquire at least modest competency in the rudiments of music: an ability to hear astutely, to read with some fluency, to understand elements and relations that make up sonic structures. But in practice there's little evidence to indicate that this is so. Nowadays not only among laymen and amateurs, but among music students and even among so-called professional musicians, there is a notable shortage of capabilities that once were taken for granted as *sine qua non* components: the musician's prerequisite equipment.

But whatever may be darkly implied thereby, the present publication seems resplendent. Of all possible prefatory blurbs, none is likely to be more informative than this truth: Marta Ghezzo here provides a work that works. I say this with confident knowledge because I've been a witness during its many tests under fire: in classrooms populated by students of distinctly different interests and levels of prior achievement. The results invariably have seemed to me akin to miracle-making. As a particular example, I cite the case of a young soprano who at first—not atypically—was scarcely able to decode the musical language of anything composed after about 1860, but who, thanks to diligent exploration of the pages that follow, was soon aurally at home in Schönberg and Webern, and thereafter became a professional performer able to master even the newest and most refractory compositions. Or, again, I recall the Ghanaian student whose expert grasp of western tonal systems was developed directly as a consequence of his work with these materials. One needs no more persuasive testimonials, I should think.

All that needs to be emphasized—and it is a point of incalculably great significance—is that Marta Ghezzo has somehow managed to bring the full power of a venerable teaching-learning art forward from Guido's tenth century to our 1970s, and to do so by broadening and deepening approaches to both past and present musical vocabularies. Students and teachers ought to line the avenues of approach and cheer this singular accomplishment. For my own part, it's a pleasure to recommend a book that responds so elegantly to so urgent a need.

MEL POWELL

Solfège, Ear Training,
Rhythm, Dictation, and
Music Theory

Introduction

Overview

Professional understanding of musical text depends on the extent of a musician's expertise in interrelated musical disciplines: solfège (sight singing), dictation, harmony, counterpoint, form and analysis, orchestration, music history. Although each of these areas comprises a particular specialization, theory, solfège, and dictation are the most fundamental and develop the complex aptitudes of the student as to ear, rhythm, musical memory, and sensitivity.

In the process of music training, it must be constantly held in mind that, at the present time, students are in touch with a contemporary music based on innovative techniques of atonality, serialism, aleatorism, and other methods of composition. It is only reasonable that they ask, "How we can understand and perform this kind of music?"

The purpose of this book is to build a thorough foundation for understanding, hearing, and performing music, starting from the tonal and progressing to the chromatic, modal, and atonal systems in a step-by-step evolution from the simple to the complex.

Content Format

The multidimensional abilities of students are developed by informing them about theoretical subjects, which are first emphasized in ear-training and rhythmic exercises, then enlarged in the solfèges, and finally reinforced by dictation. This progression represents the sequence of explanation included in each lesson—a manner of organizing these activities that permits the book to be used for individual student practice as well as for teaching purposes. Hence, the exercises are designed to involve the instructor optionally.

The method embodied in this book has been personally verified in classroom application. From the very beginning, our students develop their musical aptitudes through a well-organized process whereby they acquire a mastery of traditional techniques as well as an understanding of the phenomena that are currently evolving in contemporary music.

In regard to the theoretical subjects included in this book, an attempt has been made to present a concentrated yet thorough analysis of both traditional and contemporary theory, providing the student with a versatile musical background. In this way, later, as a performer, composer, or musicologist, he will have reasonable criteria for preferences in repertoire and style.

The ear-training exercises represent an important part of each lesson and involve the student in the process of correlating internal hearing with singing and identifying pitch tones. These exercises advance step by step, and allow the student sufficient time to assimilate all new information.

The student's progressive development of a sense of rhythm is fostered by the rhythmic exercises, which are based on the continuous addition of new formulas to previously studied rhythmic patterns.

The solfège is presented as a synthesis of pitch and rhythm and is based on the preceding ear-training and rhythmic exercises. The solfèges included in this book have been carefully designed to allow the possibility of applying any of the methods of this technique with regard to the articulation of tones: alphabetical names, numbers, or the "fixed *do*" and "movable *do*" systems based on syllables *(do, re, mi, etc.)*.

The use of syllables is a technique that facilitates the pronunciation of notes no matter how complicated their formulas or their applied system of intonation. However, syllables are important only as a means of naming the notes. They have no power to determine the internal organization of sonorous material, which can be tonal, chromatic, modal, or atonal.

Dictation, the final part of each lesson, reinforces all previous activities. It is one of the most important aspects of musical training. It begins with the abstract perception of tones and results in concrete, graphic representation.

Style

The exercises herein have not been designed merely for the purposes of developing technical competence. It is true that the study of a piece or even a solfège begins with an understanding of the technical elements of pitch and rhythm. But this is only the first step. The interpretation of each solfège must be correlated with the various styles that have been continuously evolving in the field of music.

Because style is a subject of vast range and complexity, this introduction will give a preliminary discussion of style only in terms of the exercises included herein. Any wider presentation would be beyond the scope of this book.

Style in musical performance involves a thorough understanding of the historical period of a work, whether it is *preclassic, classic, romantic, modern,* or *contemporary;* the composer's aims; and the content of the work in terms of tempo, melody, and rhythm. The character of the piece— lyric, dramatic, narrative, etc.—is expressed by applying appropriate phrasing and tone color.

For example, the performance of solfège 68 can be characterized by the *plain style (canto spinato),* which requires simplicity in performance, evenness of tone, smooth execution, and finished phrasing. The *parlando style* of solfège 136 requires the clear articulation used in "speaking," along with a free interpretation of tempo and execution. The *declamatory style* of solfège 162 is characterized by distinctively dramatic singing. The brilliant *floride style* of solfège 142 demands a very precise execution of rapid passages with a light, spare voice. This style often involves ornaments.

Tempo and expression marks at the beginning of each solfège must be carefully observed because they also indicate the character of the piece. For instance, the term *allegro scherzando* indicates the playful, light execution of solfège 105. In contrast, the term *lamento* indicates the sadness of solfège 84. The solfège 117, *Cantilène*, is sung with pure but expressive tone, and employs the swelling and receding expression of *messa di voce* and the gliding tones of *portamento*. Again, in contrast, the exercise *Versions* uses the contemporary expression of vocal effects such as tongue click, laughing, whistling, etc., designed to convey, without exaggeration, a tense and impressive manner.

Recommendations to the instructor

- The order of ear-training and rhythmic exercises is flexible, but they should come after the theoretical explanation of the topics of each lesson. Exercises for recognition of chords are intended to be used for distinguishing the included tones. Each chord is treated individually, without reference to their intercorrelation, which forms the basis of a harmony class. Ear-training exercises using intervals and chords are suggested for each lesson, and the number that will be applied depends on the number of students. At the end of many of the lessons, the instructor is given the opportunity to create a series of exercises in addition to those provided in the text.

- Chromatic elements are introduced in some of the solfèges of The Tonal System (Part One) in order, by means of increasingly difficult intonation problems, to facilitate the exercises of The Chromatic System (Part Two). The syllables used for the articulation of the chromatic notes are not changed in the "fixed *do*" system; however, in the "movable *do*" system these are changed according to the explication given below:

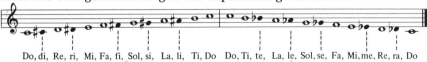

Do, di, Re, ri, Mi, Fa, fi, Sol, si, La, li, Ti, Do   Do, Ti, te, La, le, Sol, se, Fa, Mi, me, Re, ra, Do

- Exercises based on chromatic scales should be studied in small fragments—slowly, and repeated several times—with or without the rhythmic design, in order to have students initially realize the correct pitch intonation.

- Individual or group repetition is an effective method for establishing new rhythmic formulas.

- When possible, the instructor should demonstrate most of the solfèges; hearing skilled performance combining technique and feeling will develop students' sensitivity.

- If the dictation presents any difficulties to the students, first play the pitches without regard to rhythm, then apply the rhythm. Do not play more than two or three measures at a time. After finishing the dictation, it is useful to have the student sing it, following the indicated tempo and dynamic marks.

• In special situations, as when students are making quicker than average progress, the instructor can use more than one lesson for each meeting.

• Excerpts from music literature illustrating the tonal, chromatic, modal, and atonal systems are included under "Musical Examples for Further Reference" (pp. 229–59).

Recommendations to the Student

• When doing ear-training exercises to recognize pitch tones, intervals, and chords, first try to hear the tones internally; then reproduce them by singing; and finally identify them by name.

• Practice the solfèges in small fragments, then connect the fragments. Respect the indicated tempo and dynamic marks. Do not use an instrument as a permanent support, but only for the purpose of verification.

• Memorize the fragment of the dictation that is to be written down. Then write the pitch of tones, and finally apply the rhythm.

• As a comprehension device, major musical terms appear in capital letters while additional-information terms are in bold italics. This format is useful for quick reference and review purposes.

In addition to these recommendations, in order to reach professional status, it is essential to respect the *value of continuous practice* and the *necessity of being self-demanding* in all musical activities. These two factors, above all others, will foster the development of the musical aptitudes and abilities needed first simply to understand a score, and then to discover a sense of the *music* that is behind the words, signs, and notations.

MARTA A. GHEZZO

Summation of Lesson Plans

PART ONE
THE TONAL SYSTEM

Lesson	Page	Theory	Ear training	Rhythm	Solfège	Dictation
1	18	1. Musical sound 2. Generalities concerning staff notation	Recognition of tones at different pitches. Exercise for intonation.	—	—	1
2	21	1. Note-values and rests 2. The $\frac{4}{2}$ measure	—		—	2 (Rhythmic dictation)
3	24	1. Scale of "C" Major 2. Scale degrees	Exercise for intonation. Recognition of tones at different pitches.	S.E.	1–4	3

NOTE: S.E. = Similar exercises applied to new subjects.

Lesson	Page	Theory	Ear training	Rhythm	Solfège	Dictation
4	27	1. Simple accidentals 2. Relative scales 3. Scale of "a" minor	S.E.	♫ ♫	5–9	4
5	30	The Intervals: prime, second, third	Recognition of intervals	S.E.	10–12	5
6	33	The intervals: fourth, fifth	S.E.	♪ ♫	13–16	6
7	35	The intervals: sixth, seventh, octave	S.E.	S.E.	17–21	7
8	38	1. Augmented and diminished intervals 2. Inversion of intervals	S.E.	S.E.	22–26	8
9	41	1. Compound intervals 2. The upbeat	Recognition of compound intervals.	♩	27–29	9
10	44	1. The bass clef 2. The dot and the tie 3. The 3/4 measure	Exercises for intonation. Recognition of intervals.	♩ ♩	30–32	10

11	47	1. Systems of forming Major scales on different tones: scale of "G" Major 2. Tempo marks	S.E.	S.E.	33–39	11
12	52	1. Systems of forming minor scales on various tones: scale of "e" minor 2. Dynamic marks 3. Expression marks	S.E.	S.E.	40–43	12
13	57	1. Scale of "F" Major $\frac{4}{4}$ 2. The 4 measure	S.E.	Combina-tions between rests and note-values.	44–46	13
14	60	1. Scale of "d" minor 2. Generalities about the chords: the major triad	Exercises for intona-tion. Recognition of triads.	S.E.	47–50	14
15	65	1. Scale of "D" Major 2. Syncopation	S.E.	♪ ♩ ♪	51–55	15
16	69	1. Scale of "b" minor 2. The minor triad	S.E.	♫ ♫	56–58	16

Lesson	Page	Theory	Ear training	Rhythm	Solfège	Dictation
17	72	1. Scale of "B♭" Major 2. The triplet	S.E.	♫ [rhythmic notation]	59–61	17
18	75	1. Scale of "g" minor 2. The diminished triad	S.E.	[rhythmic notation]	62–65	18
19	79	1. The $\frac{2}{8}$ and $\frac{3}{8}$ measures 2. The augmented triad	S.E.	[rhythmic notation] Alternative measures.	66–70	19
20	82	1. Scale of "A" Major 2. The $\frac{4}{8}$ measure	S.E.	[rhythmic notation]	71–74	20
21	85	1. Scale of "f♯" minor 2. Articulation	S.E.	[rhythmic notation]	75–77	21
22	89	1. Scale of "E♭" Major 2. The $\frac{2}{2}$ $\frac{3}{2}$ $\frac{4}{2}$ measures	S.E.	‖	78–80	22
23	92	1. Scale of "c" minor 2. Six-beat $\frac{6}{4}$ $\frac{6}{8}$ $\frac{6}{16}$ measures	S.E.	[rhythmic notation] etc.	81–83	23

24	96	1. Scales of "E" Major and "c#" minor 2. Nine-beat 9 9 9 measures: 4 8 16	S.E.	[rhythmic notation]	84–87	24
25	100	1. Scales of "A♭" Major and "f" minor 2. Twelve-beat 12 12 12 measures: 4 8 16	S.E.	II	88–90	25
26	108	1. Scales of "B" Major and "g#" minor 2. Double accidentals	S.E.	[rhythmic notation]	91–96	26
27	104	1. Scales of "D♭" Major and "b♭" minor 2. Generalities about the seventh chords: the dominant seventh chord	S.E. Recognition of dominant seventh chord.	[rhythmic notation]	97–100	27
28	112	1. Scales of "F#" Major and "d#" minor 2. The sextuplet	S.E.	[rhythmic notation]	101–103	28
29	116	1. Scales of "G♭" Major and "e♭" minor 2. The five-beat measures: 5 5 5 4 8 16	S.E.	Combinations between rhythmic formulas	104–106	29

Lesson	Page	Theory	Ear training	Rhythm	Solfège	Dictation
30	121	1. Scales of "C#" Major and "a#" minor 2. The seven-beat 7 7 7 measures: 4 8 16	S.E. Review of intervals	S.E.	107–109	30
31	126	1. Scales of "C♭" Major and "a♭" minor 2. Variants of the Major scale 3. Table of Major and minor diatonic scales	S.E. Review of chords	S.E.	110–113	31

PART TWO
THE CHROMATIC SYSTEM

Lesson	Page	Theory	Ear training	Rhythm	Solfège	Dictation
32	134	1. Diatonic and chromatic semitones 2. Closely related keys 3. The tonal chromaticization of the Major scale	Exercises for intonation.	Combinations between rhythmic formulas	114–116	32
33	138	1. Closely related keys (continued) 2. The tonal chromaticization of the minor scale	S.E.	S.E.	117–119	33

34	141	1. Atonal chromatic-ization 2. Enharmonics	S.E.		120–123	34
35	145	1. Modulation 2. The diminished seventh chord	S.E. Recognition of chords.	♩ ♩ ♩	124–127	35

PART THREE
THE MODAL SYSTEM

SECTION A - Pentatonic scales (modes)

36	150	1. Pentatonic scale: Anhemitonic 2. The eight-beat 8 8 measures: 8 16	Exercises for intona-tion.	♫ ♫ ♫ ♫ ♫ ♫	128–130	36
37	154	1. Pentatonic scale: Hemitonic 2. Abbreviations	S.E.	♪ ♪ ♪ etc.	131–133	37

SECTION B - Medieval modes

38	159	1. Medieval modes: Ionian, Dorian 2. Ornaments	S.E.		134–136	38

Lesson	Page	Theory	Ear training	Rhythm	Solfège	Dictation
39	165	1. Medieval modes: Phrygian, Lydian 2. The duplet	S.E.	♩ ♩ ♫	137–139	39
40	169	1. Medieval modes: Mixolydian, Aeolian, Locrian 2. Seventh chords	S.E. Recognition of seventh chords.	S.E.	140–143	40
41	174	1. Chromatic modes: Ionian 2. Seventh chords (continued)	S.E.	♫ ♫	144–146	41
42	178	1. Chromatic modes: Lydian, Mixolydian 2. Ninth chords	S.E. Recognition of ninth chords.	♫	147–149	42
SECTION C - Modern and Contemporary modes						
43	182	1. Whole-tone scale 2. Eleventh chords	S.E. Recognition of eleventh chords.	♫	150–152	43
44	186	1. Messiaen's modes: First, Second, Third 2. The quintuplet	S.E.	♬ ♬	153–155	44

			S.E.		
45	191	1. Messiaen's modes: Fourth, Fifth 2. Thirteenth chords	S.E. Recognition of 13th chords.	156–158	45
46	194	Messiaen's modes: Sixth, Seventh	S.E. Review of 7th, 9th, 11th and thirteenth chords.	159–161	46

PART FOUR
THE ATONAL SYSTEM

47	200	1. "Free" atonality 2. The quadruplet 3. Chords by fourths	Exercises for intonation. Recognition of chords by fourths.	162–166	47
48	205	Serial music	Exercises for intonation based on serial technique.	167–170	48
49	210	1. Serial music (continued) 2. Chords by seconds	S.E. Recognition of chords by seconds. Exclusion of time signature.	171–173	49

Lesson	Page	Theory	Ear training	Rhythm	Solfège	Dictation
50	215	Aleatory music	Aleatory exercises for rhythm and pitch.		174–176	50
51	220	Aleatory music: graphic symbols	Aleatory exercises based on graphic symbols.		177–178	51

PART ONE
The Tonal System

Lesson 1

1. Musical Sound
2. Generalities Concerning Staff Notation

1. Although a boundless variety of sound envelops us, the field of acoustics recognizes two distinctive categories: MUSICAL SOUND, which results from regular vibrations per second; and NOISE, which results from irregular vibrations.

Musical sound has four essential qualities:

- PITCH—the number of vibrations per second
- DURATION—the extent in time of such vibrations
- INTENSITY—the amplitude of the vibrations
- TIMBRE—the characteristic quality of a musical sound resulting from the number of overtones produced by partial vibrations of a sonorous object

2. In consequence of a long historical process, the written representation of musical sound consists of the interrelated use of certain graphic notations:

- STAFF—Five horizontal, parallel lines with four equally distanced spaces between them, which are counted upward. For representation above or below the staff, *ledger lines* are used.

Ex. 1

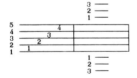

- CLEFS—Establish the pitch position of notes on the staff:

The treble clef:
  (G clef)

The bass clef:
  (F clef)

The C clefs:

• SYSTEM OF NOTATION—Generally, two systems of notation, the *alphabetic* and *the syllabic*, are used to identify and distinguish tones.

—*Alphabetic*—the tones are identified by the use of roman letters: c, d, e, f, g, a, b, c

—*Syllabic*—the tones are identified by syllables: do, re, mi, fa, sol, la, ti, introduced by Guido d'Arezzo (c.995–1050):

Ex. 2

Alphabetic: c   d   e   f   g   a   b   c
Syllabic: do, re, mi, fa, sol, la, ti, do

NOTE: There are two methods of applying Guido's syllables to scale degrees:
  a. The "fixed *do*"—*do* indicates the pitch of "c" regardless of the key
  b. The "movable *do*"—*do* represents the tonic, which is the first step of a major scale.
      Ex. In the key of G Major, G = do. In the key of E Major, E = do.
      In the minor scales "la" represents the Tonic.
      Ex. In the key of e minor, e = la. In the key of d minor, d = la.

• REGISTER—Results from the levels of pitch given to the above seven tones and generates the following *system of octaves:*

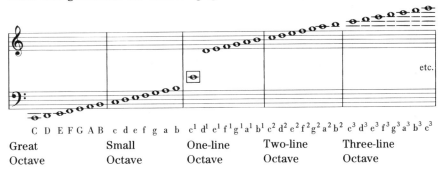

C D E F G A B c d e f g a b $c^1 d^1 e^1 f^1 g^1 a^1 b^1$ $c^2 d^2 e^2 f^2 g^2 a^2 b^2$ $c^3 d^3 e^3 f^3 g^3 a^3 b^3 c^3$

Great   Small   One-line   Two-line   Three-line
Octave   Octave   Octave   Octave   Octave

Ear-training exercises

  a. Exercises for intonation: Keep regular beats, but hold the notes that are marked by the *fermata* (*It.,* ⌢):

1.

2.

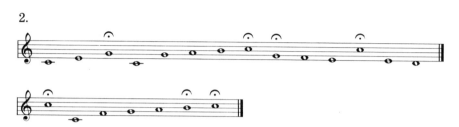

b. Starting from the given note, identify the name of the tones played by the instructor (Use of the piano is recommended):

LA

Dictation 1

Lesson 2

1. Note-Values and Rests
2. The $\frac{2}{4}$ Measure

1. The duration of a sound is represented by a complex system of notation mainly consisting of note values and rests.

 • NOTE VALUES—indicate the length of time that a note is played or sung, while the RESTS are their equivalent in silence.

Ex. 3	Whole	Half	Quarter	Eighth	Six-teenth	Thirty-second	Sixty-fourth
Note-values	𝅝	𝅗𝅥	♩	♪	𝅘𝅥𝅯	𝅘𝅥𝅰	𝅘𝅥𝅱
Rests							
Duration in beats	4	2	1	1/2	1/16	1/32	1/64

 • METER—is the basis of the measure-system and consists of the periodical alteration of stressed and unstressed pulsations or beats. There are three types of meter:

—**Binary** or **Double**—has a stress every second beat—
2 2 2 2
and generates the 2, 4, 8, 16 measures.

—**Ternary** or **Triple**—has a stress every third beat—
3 3 3 3
and generates the 2, 4, 8, 16 measures

—**Mixed**—combines the binary and ternary meters,

Ex. 4

or

and generates the 5, 7, (9), 10, 11, 13 etc. beat measures.

2. The MEASURE is a musical fragment between two equally accented

beats delimited by **bar lines.** There are two categories of measure:
- SIMPLE MEASURES—have one **main accent** on the first beat.
- COMPOUND MEASURES—consist of two or more simple metrical

groups, with the main accent on the first beat and additional **secondary accents** on other beats.

NOTE: According to some musical theorists, simple and compound measures are based not on the number of accents, but on the nature of the note-value as a time unit. In this case, a simple measure is characterized by the absence of dotted time units while the compound is marked by their inclusion.

The $\frac{2}{4}$ MEASURE is generated by the binary meter in which the main accent occurs on the first beat and is repeated periodically every other beat.
- TIME SIGNATURE—is placed at the beginning of the staff after the clef

and includes two numbers, with the upper one indicating the number of beats and the lower signifying the note-value to be performed for each beat.

Ex. 5

etc.

The conducting pattern of $\frac{2}{4}$ measure is:

Rhythmic Exercises

NOTE: Use of conducting patterns is recommended for rhythmic exercises while pronouncing the syllables, "ta-ta."

---

c. Repeat and identify the formulas based on the rhythmic patterns above, as played by the instructor.

Dictation 2

Lesson 3

1. Scale of "C" Major
2. Scale Degrees

1. A SCALE is a step-by-step succession of seven different notes with the first note repeated at the octave. The name of the scale (C,D,E, etc.) is given by the first step while the mode (major or minor) is determined by the manner of organizing the tones and semitones.

- MAJOR SCALE—is built up on five *tones* (whole-tones) and two *semitones* (half-tones) which are located between the III and IV, and the VII and VIII steps.

Ex. 6

Scale of "C" Major

I	II	III	IV	V	V	VII	VIII	I	III	V	VIII

- ARPEGGIO—consists of successively playing the tones of a chord, as opposed to the CHORD itself, which is the simultaneous sounding of the tones. The arpeggio helps in establishing the sonority of the scale and includes the following steps: I-III-V-VIII.

2. SCALE DEGREES are names which denote both the position and function of each of the steps in a scale:
TONIC = I step
SUPERTONIC = II step
MEDIANT = III step
SUBDOMINANT = IV step
DOMINANT = V step
SUPERDOMINANT or SUBMEDIANT = VI step
SUBTONIC or LEADING TONE = VII step

NOTE: The seventh step is called "subtonic" when it is situated at a whole-step distance from the tonic, as in the natural minor scale (Lesson 4), and it is called the "leading tone" when it is situated at a half-step distance from the tonic, as in the Major scale, harmonic minor scale, etc.

Ear-Training Exercises

a. Exercises for intonation in "C" Major:

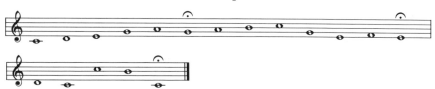

b. Starting from the given note, sing and identify the tones played by the instructor.

Rhythmic Exercises

Solfège

NOTE: For the solfèges, breathing is indicated by the symbol: '

Dictation 3

Lesson 4

1. Simple Accidentals
2. Relative Scales
3. Scale of "a" minor

1. SIMPLE ACCIDENTALS modify the pitch of a note:
- SHARP [#]—raises by one semitone
- FLAT [♭]—lowers by one semitone
- NATURAL [♮]—cancels previous accidentals

Ex. 7

2. RELATIVE SCALES—involve the same notes because of their common **key signature,** which is placed immediately after the clef. Thus, each Major scale has a relative minor scale which can be obtained by counting down three steps or a minor third from the tonic of the Major scale.* For example, "C" Major's relative scale is "a" minor.

3. The minor scales are formed on successions of tones and semitones. The place and the number of these semitones determine the **three variants** that any of the minor scales may have.

---

*NOTE: For the minor-third interval, see Lesson 5.

Scale of "a" minor

- NATURAL "a" minor—has two semitones between the II and III, and the V and VI steps.

- HARMONIC "a" minor—results from raising the VII step by one semitone, thus obtaining three semitones, between the II and III, V and VI, and VII and VIII steps. The characteristic interval of this scale is a 1-1/2-tone distance, called the **augmented second,** between the VI and VII steps.

• MELODIC "a" minor—is obtained by raising the VI and VII steps one semitone, upward, and then canceling the accidentals, downward. As a result, the positions of the semitones are between the II and III, and VII and VIII steps, upward, and between the VI and V, and the III and II steps, downward.

I II III IV V VI VII VIII VIII VII VI V IV III II I

Ear-Training Exercises

a. Exercise for intonation including the three variants of "a" minor:

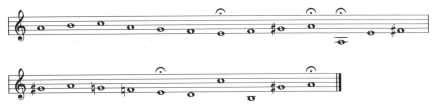

b. Starting from the given note, sing and identify the tones played by the instructor.

Rhythmic Exercises

New rhythmic formula:

Solfège

Dictation 4

Lesson 5

The Intervals: Prime, Second, Third

The INTERVAL is the distance in pitch between two notes. The name of each interval shows the number of steps included between the *lower or base* and *top* notes, determining its *quantity.* The *quality,* or internal organization of pitch distance of an interval, has two general categories: (1) perfect and (2) Major or minor. All intervals can be augmented or diminished. (See Lesson 8.)

NOTE: The term base-note, referring to the lower note of an interval or chord, is not to be confused with the vocal quality, "bass."

- The perfect PRIME, or unison, includes one step.

Ex. 8

- The SECOND, Major or minor, includes two steps.

Ex. 9

- The THIRD, Major or minor, includes three steps.

Ex. 10

NOTE:—Abbreviations used in the analysis of intervals:

T = Tone (whole-tone)
S = Semitone (half-tone)
M = Major
m = minor
p = perfect

—When the notes of an interval are played simultaneously, the interval is considered *harmonic* and when the notes are played successively, it is considered *melodic.*

Ear-Training Exercises

a. Build up and sing the prime, second, and third intervals on the following tones:

b. Sing and determine the intervals suggested below:

c. Identify by ear the following intervals played by the instructor. (Use of the piano for ear-training is recommended.)

Rhythmic Exercises

Solfège

11.

12.

Dictation 5

Lesson 6

The Intervals: Fourth, Fifth

In the concept of pitch distance, two other intervals to be considered are:

- The perfect FOURTH—includes four steps.

Ex. 11

- The perfect FIFTH—includes five steps.

Ex. 12

Ear-Training Exercises

a. Build up and sing the intervals mentioned above on the following tones:

b. Sing and determine the intervals below:

c. Identify by ear these suggested intervals played by the instructor:

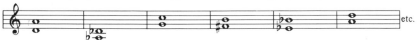

etc.

Rhythmic Exercises

New rhythmic formulas:

Solfège

Dictation 6

Lesson 7

The Intervals: Sixth, Seventh, Octave

Three final intervals conclude the examination of the concept of pitch distance:

• The SIXTH, Major or minor, includes six steps.

Ex. 13

• The SEVENTH, Major or minor, includes seven steps.

Ex. 14

• The perfect EIGHTH or OCTAVE includes eight steps.

Ex. 15

Ear-Training Exercises

a. Build up and sing the sixth, seventh, and eighth intervals on the following tones:

b. Sing and identify the intervals below:

c. Identify by ear the following intervals played by the instructor:

Rhythmic Exercises

Solfège

21.

Dictation 7

Lesson 8

1. Augmented and Diminished Intervals
2. Inversion of Intervals

1. Intervals previously mentioned (perfect, Major, and minor) can be modified, to obtain augmented and diminished intervals.

- AUGMENTED INTERVALS [+]—are obtained in two ways:
—raising the top of a perfect or Major interval by one semitone;

Ex. 16

—lowering the base note of a perfect or Major interval by one semitone.

Ex. 17

- DIMINISHED INTERVALS [−]—can be obtained from any interval except the prime, since the top of the interval can not be lower than the base note. Diminished intervals are formed in two ways:

—lowering the top of the perfect or minor interval by one semitone.

Ex. 18

—raising the base note of a perfect or minor interval by one semitone

Ex. 19  etc.

NOTE: For double accidentals, double sharps and double flats, see Lesson 26.

2. INVERSION OF INTERVALS is obtained by moving the base note of the interval to a higher octave or the top note to a lower octave. Except for the perfect intervals, an inversion changes the *quality* of all intervals, in the following ways:

—Major intervals become minor,

—minor intervals become Major,

—augmented intervals become diminished,

—diminished intervals become augmented.

Also in this process, the *quantity* of the intervals is changed. For example: The prime becomes the eighth, the second becomes the seventh, etc.

The following table may be used for reference:

1	2	3	4	5	6	7	8
8	7	6	5	4	3	2	1

Ex. 20

3M   6m   2m   7M   4p   5p   4+   5-

Ear-Training Exercises

a. Build up and sing the augmented and diminished intervals on the following tones:

b. First form and then sing the inversion of the intervals suggested below:

c. Form and sing the augmented and diminished intervals on the notes suggested by the instructor.

Rhythmic Exercises

Solfège

Dictation 8

Lesson 9

1. Compound Intervals
2. The Upbeat

1. COMPOUND INTERVALS are obtained by adding to the top of the octave any of the simple intervals from the second to the eighth. As a result of this process, the following compound intervals are obtained: ninth, tenth, eleventh, twelfth, thirteenth, fourteenth, and fifteenth, which is a double octave.

Ex. 21

These intervals can also be augmented or diminished.

Ex. 22

2. The UPBEAT or *Auftakt (Ger.)* is a note or a group of notes preceding the first complete measure of a musical composition. Often the note-values which are absent from the first, incomplete, measure are made up at the end.

Ex. (See Solfèges 27 and 29.)

Ear-Training Exercises

a. Sing each compound interval explained above. (The register may be changed.)

b. Build up and sing all compound intervals starting from the suggested notes below:

c. Identify by ear compound intervals played by the instructor:

Rhythmic Exercises

Solfège

Dictation 9

Lesson 10

1. The Bass Clef
2. The Dot and the Tie
3. The $\frac{3}{4}$ Measure

1. The BASS CLEF is placed on the fourth line of the staff, determining the pitch of "f" in the small octave.

Ex. 23

| Alphabetic: | E | F | G | A | B | C | D | E | f | g | a | b | c¹ |
| Syllabic: | MI | FA | SOL | LA | TI | DO | RE | MI | fa | sol | la | ti | do¹ |

etc.

NOTE: Capital letters indicate the notes included in the Great Octave, small letters belong to the notes from the small octave.

---

2. The DOT adds one half of its value to a note.

Ex. 24

 = 3 beats.

 = 1½ beats.

The TIE fuses the note-values of tones of the same pitch.

Ex. 25

1 + ½ beat

3. The $\frac{3}{4}$ MEASURE is based on a ternary meter, with the main accent placed on the first beat and periodically repeated after every third beat. This measure includes three beats, each of which has a quarter note as a time-unit.

Ex. 26

The conducting pattern of the $\frac{3}{4}$ measure:

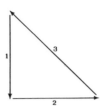

Ear-Training Exercises

  a. Exercise for intonation using the bass clef:

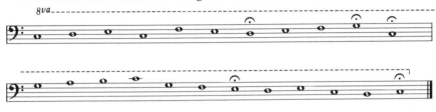

NOTE:—Exercises using the bass clef can be changed to any convenient register.
      —Abbreviations: 8 va: transpose the notes to the higher octave.
                          8 va bassa: transpose the notes to the lower octave.

---

  b. Recognition of all intervals—Major, minor and perfect—played by the instructor.

Rhythmic Exercises

Solfège

Dictation 10

Lesson 11

1. Systems of Forming Major Scales on Different Tones: Scale of "G" Major
2. Tempo Marks

1. There are three methods of constructing the Major scales:

• TRANSPOSITION OF THE BASIC PATTERN—use the "C" Major scale as a model and, keeping the sequence of tones and semitones, transpose this structure onto any other tone. The accidentals obtained from this method are called *constitutive alterations* and are placed at the beginning of the staff immediately after the clef forming the *key signature* of the scale.

Ex. 27 Transposition of "C" Major onto G results in the following tones:

Scale of "G" Major

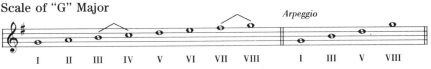

| I | II | III | IV | V | VI | VII | VIII | I | III | V | VIII |

The semitones are between the III and IV and the VII and VIII steps.

• SUCCESSION OF PERFECT FIFTH INTERVALS—construct ascending fifth intervals to obtain scales with sharps, and descending fifths to obtain scales with flats in the key signature.

Ex. 28   etc. Bb ⟵——— F ⟵——— [C] ———⟶ G ———⟶ D   etc.
                 2b   1b   1♯   2♯

• SYSTEM OF TETRACHORDS—divide a Major scale into two four-note fragments to produce lower and upper Major tetrachords. Then a new Major scale, one fifth higher in pitch, can be obtained by continuing the upper tetrachord through the addition of another Major one.

Ex. 29

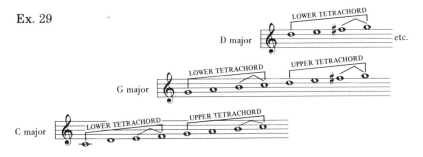

NOTE: Tetrachord (Greek = *Tetra-chordon*) means a stepwise succession of four different tones. The following tetrachords are included in the tonal system:

— Major

Ex. 30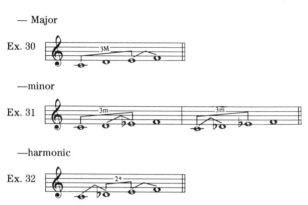

—minor

Ex. 31

—harmonic

Ex. 32

Minor and harmonic tetrachords are used to form minor scales. (See Lesson 12.)

A new Major scale which is one fifth lower can be obtained by using the same process used for the new Major scale one fifth higher by simply applying this process downward. This results in the lower tetrachord of the previous scale becoming the upper one.

2. TEMPO MARKS determine the speed of performing a composition. There are three categories of tempo marks representing the slowest to most rapid motion:

- SLOW TEMPO
    Largo = broad
    Lento = slow
    Adagio = leisurely, slow
    Larghetto = a little faster than Largo
- MEDIUM TEMPO
    Andante = walking
    Andantino = a little faster than *Andante*
    Moderato = moderate
    Allegretto = rather fast
- FAST TEMPO
    Allegro = fast
    Vivace = lively, brisk
    Presto = very fast
    Prestissimo = as fast as possible

For gradual change of speed, additional terms are used:
    rallentando (rall.) = slowing down
    ritardando (ritard.) = growing slower and slower
    ritenuto (rit.) = at a slower rate of speed
    accelerando (accel.) = growing faster
    stringendo = hastening

In case of a need to return to the preceding pace, the term *a tempo* is used. Other expressions added to the tempo marks are

molto = much, very
meno = less
mosso = moved
con = with

Ex. 33:   *Molto Allegro* = very fast
          Con stringendo = with haste

NOTE: Indications given by the **Metronome** establish the number of beats per minute.
    Ex. 34   MM. = 63—means 63 beats per minute with a quarter-note-value for each beat.

Ear-Training Exercises

a. Exercise for intonation in "G" Major:

b. Recognition of all intervals—Major, minor and perfect—played by the instructor.

Rhythmic Exercises

Solfège

Dictation 11

Lesson 12

1. Systems of Forming Minor Scales on Different Tones: Scale of "e" minor
2. Dynamic Marks
3. Expression Marks

1. The three methods mentioned in Lesson 11 are also used to form minor scales on different tones:

• TRANSPOSITION OF THE BASIC PATTERN—using the "a" minor scales as models for minors in other keys by transposing the same succession, or pattern, of tones and semitones onto other tones. The new accidentals will constitute the key signature.

Ex. 35 Transposition of "a" minor onto "e" results in the following tones:

Scale of "e" minor

—the **natural** "e" minor has semitones between the II and III and the V and VI steps.

—the **harmonic** "e" minor has semitones between the II and III, V and VI, and the VII and VIII steps.

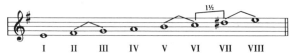

—the **melodic** "e" minor has semitones upward between the II and III and the VII and VIII steps, and downward between the VI and V and the III and II steps.

• SUCCESSION OF PERFECT FIFTH INTERVALS—construct ascending fifth intervals to obtain scales with sharps, and descending fifths to obtain scales with flats in the key signature.

Ex. 36   etc.   g ◄——— d ◄——— 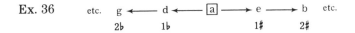 ———► e ———► b   etc.
                  2♭   1♭   a   1♯   2♯

• SYSTEM OF TETRACHORDS—transpose on different tones the tetrachords which exist in the minor scale: The minor, harmonic, and Major. (See Lesson 11.) In this process, the lower tetrachords are identical for all minor scales, and the upper ones change from one variant to another. The minor scales include the following tetrachords:

—the **natural** "a" minor:

—the **harmonic** "a" minor:

—the **melodic** "a" minor:

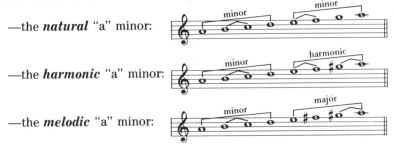

The transposition of these tetrachords onto different tones will produce new minor scales. For example, start with a minor tetrachord on "e" and continue with another one to obtain the natural "e" minor scale.

Ex. 37

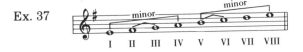

I   II   III   IV   V   VI   VII   VIII

NOTE: Since the last method explained is the most complicated, the first two procedures are recommended for forming minor scales on different tones.

---

2. DYNAMIC MARKS (terms, signs, abbreviations) indicate the intensity of a musical sound. The most frequently used marks are the following:

pianissimo (pp) = very soft
piano (p) = soft
mezzo piano (mp) = half-soft
mezzo forte (mf) = half loud
forte (f) = loud, strong
fortissimo (ff) = very loud

For gradual change of volume, the following terms are used:

crescendo (cresc.) < = increasing in loudness
decrescendo (decresc.) > = decreasing in loudness

Besides the basic dynamic marks, additional terms are used:

assai = very   *poco* = little
più = more   Ex. 38 *piu forte* = louder

3. EXPRESSION MARKS indicate the general feeling of the music. The manner of using these varies from one performer to another. In the application of these terms, it is necessary to respect the style of the musical composition. Currently, the following terms are used:

agitato = agitated
soave = suavely, flowingly
tranquillo = quietly
scherzando = playfully, jestingly
morendo = dying away
risoluto = vigorous
giocoso = playfully, merrily
lamentoso = plaintively, mournfully
deciso = decided, energic
volante = flying, light
cantabile = in singing style
animato = vivaciously, spiritedly
grazioso = gracefully, elegantly
leggiero = light, airy
con spirito = with spirit
con delicatezza = with delicacy
con allegrezza = with liveliness, rapidly
con brio = with fire and dash
con moto = with an animated movement

Ear-Training Exercises

a. Exercise for intonation including the three variants of "e" minor:

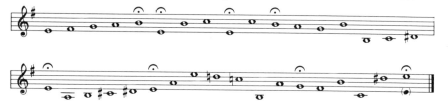

b. Recognition of all intervals—Major, minor, and perfect—played by the instructor.

Rhythmic Exercises

Solfège

Dictation 12

Lesson 13

1. Scale of "F" Major

2. The $\frac{4}{4}$ Measure

1. As a result of respecting the Major scale structure, the SCALE of "F" MAJOR includes the following tones:

Scale of "F" Major

The semitones are between the III and IV and the VII and VIII steps.

NOTE: Beginning with this lesson, for more theoretical explanation of the Major scales, see Lessons 3 and 11.

---

2. The $\frac{4}{4}$ MEASURE [C] is based on two binary meters and consists of four beats in one measure with a quarter-note-value as the time-unit.

The $\frac{4}{4}$ measure includes two accents repeated periodically:
— the ***main accent*** on the first beat
— the ***secondary accent*** on the third beat

Ex. 39

The conducting pattern for $\frac{4}{4}$ measure is:

Ear-Training Exercises

a. Exercise for intonation in "F" Major:

b. Recognition of all intervals—Major, minor, and perfect—played by the instructor.

Rhythmic Exercises

Solfège

Dictation 13

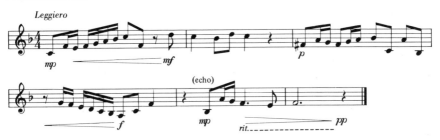

Lesson 14

1. Scale of "d" minor
2. Generalities about the Chords: The Major Triad

1. "d" MINOR is the relative scale of "F" Major—both have the same key-signature and they use the same tones.

Scale of "d" minor

— the **natural** "d" minor has semitones between the II and III and the V and VI steps.

I II III IV V VI VII VIII I III V VIII

—the **harmonic** "d" minor has semitones between the II and III, V and VI, and VII and VIII steps.

I II III IV V VI VII VIII

—the **melodic** "d" minor has semitones upward between the II and III and the VII and VIII steps, and downward between the VI and V and the III and II steps.

I II III IV V VI VII VIII VIII VII VI V IV III II I

NOTE: If more explanation is needed, review lessons 4 and 12.

---

2. The CHORD is the simultaneous sounding of two or more tones. When a chord consists of three tones superimposed at intervals of thirds, it is called a TRIAD.

The three **elements** of a triad are
—Fifth
—Third
—Root

Ex. 40

The distances between these elements generate the *four kinds of triad:*

- MAJOR

Ex. 41

- MINOR

Ex. 42

- DIMINISHED

Ex. 43

- AUGMENTED

Ex. 44

Depending on which element is the lowest, or base note, the chord can appear as the root position or either of two inversions:

—the *root position,* with the root as the lowest, or base note, marked by $\frac{5}{3}$

—the *first inversion,* with the third as the lowest, or base note, marked by $\frac{6}{3}$

—the *second inversion* with the fifth as the lowest, or base note, marked by $\frac{6}{4}$

NOTE: The numbers indicate the superimposed intervals of the triad.

Ex. 45

The Major Triad

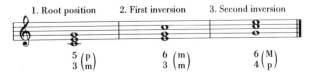

Ear-Training Exercises

a. Exercises for intonation in "d" minor:

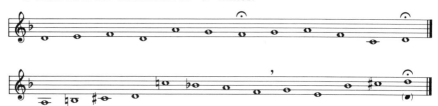

b. Starting from the base note, build up and sing the root position of the four kinds of triad on the following notes:

c. Form and sing the Major triad in root position and inversions starting on the suggested notes below:

d. Identify by ear the following triads played by the instructor:

etc.

Rhythmic Exercises

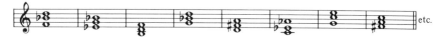

a. (rhythmic notation)

b. (rhythmic notation)

Solfège

47. Cantabile

Dictation 14

Lesson 15

1. Scale of "D" Major
2. Syncopation

1. The SCALE of "D" MAJOR includes the following tones:

The semitones are between the III and IV and the VII and VIII steps.

2. SYNCOPATION is an irregular rhythmic pattern which results from connecting a strong beat with the previous weak beat. This causes a shift of accent from the strong to the weak beat.

Ex. 46

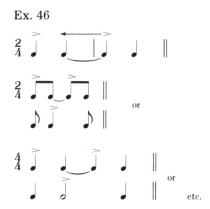

Often in musical practice, the notes that are tied together have different note-values.

Ex. 47

Ear-Training Exercises

a. Exercise for intonation in "D" Major:

b. Sing and identify the following triads:

c. Form and sing the four kinds of triad in root position on the notes suggested below:

d. Exercise for recognition of Major triads in root position and inversions played by the instructor:

Rhythmic Exercises

Solfège

Dictation 15

Lesson 16

1. Scale of "b" minor
2. The Minor Triad

1. "b" MINOR is the relative scale of "D" Major, inasmuch as both have the same key signature and they use the same tones.

Scale of "b" minor

—the **natural** "b" minor, with semitones between the II and III and the V and VI steps.

—the **harmonic** "b" minor, with semitones between the II and III, V and VI, and VII and VIII steps.

—the **melodic** "b" minor, with semitones upward between the II and III and the VII and VIII steps, and downward between the VI and V and the III and II steps.

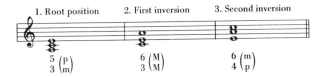

2. As in the previous explanation of chords (Lesson 14), the MINOR TRIAD has the root position as well as two inversions:

Ear-Training Exercises

a. Exercise for intonation in "b" minor:

b. Build up and sing the root position and inversions on the minor triad on the following notes:

c. Sing and identify the following minor triads:

d. Identify by ear the following minor triads played by the instructor:

Rhythmic Exercises

New rhythmic formulas: ♩ = ♫ ♪

♩. ♪ or ♪ ♩.

a. 2/4 ...

b. 3/4 ...

Solfège

NOTE: Mazurka—a Polish national dance in triple meter, of moderate speed, generally based on the following rhythmic pattern:

Dictation 16

Lesson 17

1. Scale of "B♭" Major
2. The Triplet

1. The SCALE OF "B♭" MAJOR includes the following tones:

The semitones are between the III and IV and the VII and VIII steps.

2. The TRIPLET is a group of three equal notes performed in the time usually allotted to two notes of the same value. The triplet is marked by the number 3 and either a legato [⌣] or bracket [⎣⎦] above or below the formula.

Ex. 48

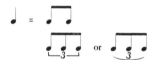

By connecting two notes from this basic pattern, the following formulas are accomplished:

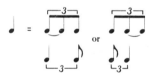

Ear-Training Exercises

a. Exercise for intonation in "B♭" Major:

b. Sing and identify the following triads:

c. Exercise for the recognition of Major and minor triads in root position and inversions played by the instructor:

etc.

Rhythmic Exercises

Solfège

Dictation 17

Lesson 18

1. Scale of "g" minor
2. The Diminished Triad

1. "g" MINOR is the relative scale of "B♭" Major—both have the same key signature and they use the same tones.

Scale of "g" minor

—the **natural** "g" minor has semitones between the II and III and the V and VI steps.

I   II III IV V VI VII VIII   I   III V VIII

—the **harmonic** "g" minor has semitones between the II and III, V and VI, and VII and VIII steps.

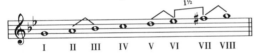

I   II   III   IV   V   VI   VII VIII

—the **melodic** "g" minor has semitones upward between the II and III and the VII and VIII steps, and downward between the VI and V and the III and II steps.

I II III IV V VI VII VIII VIII VII VI V IV III II I

2. The name of the DIMINISHED TRIAD is derived from the diminished fifth interval which occurs in the root position between the root and the fifth of the chord. This triad also has two inversions.

Ex. 49

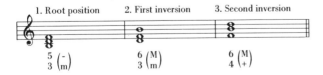

1. Root position   2. First inversion   3. Second inversion

$\begin{smallmatrix}5\\3\end{smallmatrix}\left(\begin{smallmatrix}-\\m\end{smallmatrix}\right)$ $\begin{smallmatrix}6\\3\end{smallmatrix}\left(\begin{smallmatrix}M\\m\end{smallmatrix}\right)$ $\begin{smallmatrix}6\\4\end{smallmatrix}\left(\begin{smallmatrix}M\\+\end{smallmatrix}\right)$

Ear-Training Exercises

a. Exercise for intonation in "g" minor:

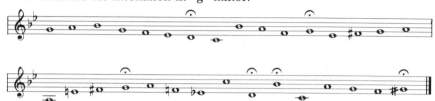

b. Starting from the base note, form and sing the root position and inversions of the diminished triad on the notes suggested below:

c. Sing and identify the following diminished triads:

d. Identify the following triads played by the instructor:

Rhythmic Exercises

Solfège

Grazioso ben ritmato M.M. ♩ = 78

65.

Dictation 18

Moderato

Lesson 19

1. The $\frac{2}{8}$ and $\frac{3}{8}$ Measures
2. The Augmented Triad

1. The $\frac{2}{8}$ and $\frac{3}{8}$ MEASURES include two and three beats respectively, with an eighth note as the time-unit. The accent falls on the first beat of each measure and is periodically repeated.

Ex. 50

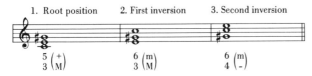

The measures mentioned above use the same conducting patterns as the $\frac{2}{4}$ and $\frac{3}{4}$ measures, only the time-unit being changed.

2. The name of the AUGMENTED TRIAD is derived from the augmented fifth interval which occurs in the root position between the root and the fifth of the chord. This triad also has two inversions.

Ex. 51

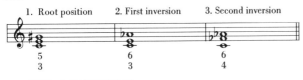

NOTE: It is important to observe that in this triad the sonorous effect of the root position and inversions is identical.

Ex.

1. Root position   2. First inversion   3. Second inversion

5   6   6
3   3   4

Ear-Training Exercises

a. Starting from the base note, construct and sing the augmented triads on the notes below:

b. Sing and identify the following triads:

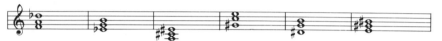

c. Form and sing augmented triads in root position and inversions on the notes indicated by the instructor.

Rhythmic Exercises

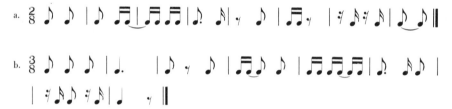

Solfège

NOTE: Solfège 70 is based on **alternating** or **multimeter measures**—a succession or alternation of differing meter measures.

Dictation 19

Lesson 20

1. Scale of "A" Major
2. The 8/4 Measure

1. The SCALE of "A" MAJOR includes the following tones:

The semitones are between the III and IV and the VII and VIII steps.

2. The 4/8 MEASURE is based on two binary meters, both of which have the eighth note as a time-unit. This measure includes two accents which are periodically repeated:

—the **main accent** on the first beat.
—the **secondary accent** on the third beat.

Ex. 52

The conducting pattern is similar to the 4/4 measure, only the time-unit being changed.

Ear-Training Exercises

a. Exercise for intonation in "A" Major:

b. Build up and sing the four kinds of triad in root position and inversions on the following tones:

c. Exercise for recognition of triads in root position and inversions played by the instructor:

Rhythmic Exercises

New rhythmic formulas:

Solfège

Dictation 20

Lesson 21

1. Scale of "f#" minor
2. Articulation

1. "f#" MINOR is the relative scale of "A" Major. They share the same key signature and tones.

Scale of "f#" minor

—the *natural* "f#" minor has semitones between the II and III and the V and VI steps.

—the *harmonic* "f#" minor has semitones between the II and III, V and VI, and VII and VIII steps.

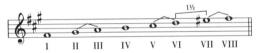

—the *melodic* "f#" minor has semitones upward between the II and III and the VII and VIII steps, and downward between the VI and V and the III and II steps.

2. ARTICULATION involves various means of giving a distinctive quality to the performance of notes and is marked by a series of symbols:

legato ⌒ = play with no break between the notes

legato staccato = half legato

staccato = detached, separated

tenuto or ten. = sustained

sforzando *sfz* , and *sforzato* *sf* = stressed, forced

Ear-Training Exercises

a. Exercise for intonation in "f#" minor:

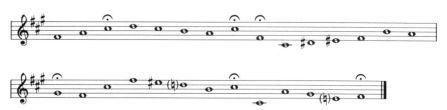

b. Exercise for recognition of triads in root position and inversions in different registers, as played by the instructor:

Ex. 53

Rhythmic Exercises

Solfège

NOTE: Bolero, a Spanish dance in triple time, of moderate tempo, is based on the following rhythmic formulas:

Dictation 21

Lesson 22

1. Scale of "E♭" Major
      2 3 4
2. The 2, 2, 2 Measures.

1. The SCALE of "E♭" MAJOR consists of the following tones:

The semitones are between the III and IV and the VII and VIII steps.

     2 3   4
2. The 2, 2 and 2 MEASURES all have a half note-value as their denominator or time-unit. These measures also have a ***main accent*** on
                       4
the first beat. In addition, the 2 measure has a ***secondary accent*** on the third beat.

Ex. 54

The conducting patterns of the measures mentioned above are similar to
                                        2 3 4
the previously explained 2, 3, and 4 beat measures (4, 4, 4) only the time-unit being changed.

Ear-Training Exercises

a. Exercise for intonation in "E♭" Major:

b. Continue the exercise below: Starting on the same note, first form and then sing all the triads in root position and inversions:

c. Exercise for recognition of triads in root position and inversions in different registers as played by the instructor.

Rhythmic Exercises

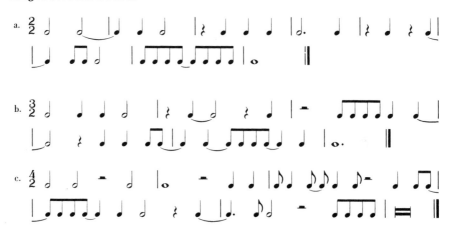

NOTE: Brevis [◫]—a note equal in value to two whole-notes (o‿o) used in medieval and Renaissance notation.

Solfège

Dictation 22

Lesson 23

1. Scale of "c" minor

$$\overset{6}{4} \quad \overset{6}{8} \quad \overset{6}{16}$$

2. Six-Beat Measures: 4, 8, 16

1. "c" MINOR is the relative scale of "E♭" Major, inasmuch as both have the same key signature and tones.

Scale of "c" minor

—the **natural** "c" minor has semitones between the II and III and the V and VI steps.

—the **harmonic** "c" minor has semitones between the II and III, the V and VI, and the VII and VIII steps.

—the **melodic** "c" minor has semitones upward between the II and III and VII and VIII steps, and downward between the VI and V and the III and II steps.

2. Compound SIX-BEAT MEASURES are based on two ternary meters. Thus, there are two accents, repeated periodically in each measure:
—the **main accent** on the first beat
—the **secondary accent** on the fourth beat.

Ex. 55

The conducting patterns are:
    fast or moderate tempo   slow tempo

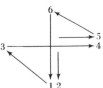

Ear-Training Exercises

    a. Exercise for intonation including the variants of "c" minor:

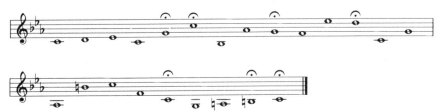

    b. Build up and sing the four kinds of triads in root position and inversions, starting from the same note:

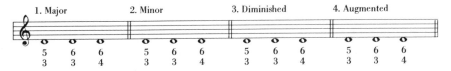

    c. Exercise for recognition of triads in root position and inversions in different registers as played by the instructor.

Rhythmic Exercise

a.

b.

c.

Solfège

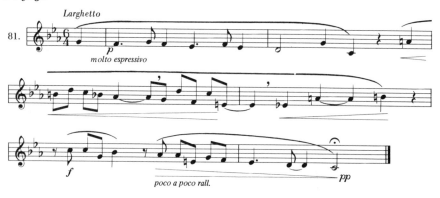

81.

Larghetto

p

molto espressivo

f

poco a poco rall.

pp

82.

Allegretto

p

mf

f

mp

Dictation 23

Lesson 24

1. Scales of "E" Major and "c#" minor

2. Nine-Beat Measures: $\overset{9}{4}$, $\overset{9}{8}$, $\overset{9}{16}$

1. "E" MAJOR and "c#" MINOR are relative scales. Both have the same key signature and use the same tones.

Scale of "E" Major

The semitones are between the III and IV and the VII and VIII steps.

Scale of "c#" minor

—the *natural* "c#" minor has semitones between the II and III and the V and VI steps.

—the *harmonic* "c#" minor has semitones between the II and III, and the V and VI, and the VII and VIII steps.

—the *melodic* "c#" minor has semitones upward between the II and III and the VII and VIII steps, and downward between the VI and V and the III and II steps.

NOTE: Since the focus of the previous lessons has been the development of the student's ability to analyze, hear, and sing various scales, beginning with this lesson, the Major and its relative minor scale will now be treated together. For a more detailed theoretical explanation of Major and minor scales, see Lessons 3 and 4.

2. Compound NINE-BEAT MEASURES consist of three ternary meters. There are three accents, periodically repeated in each measure:
—the ***main accent*** on the first beat
—the ***secondary accents*** on the fourth and the seventh beats

Ex. 56

The conducting patterns are:
    fast or moderate tempo   slow tempo

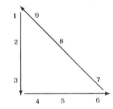 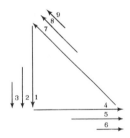

Ear-Training Exercises

   a. Exercise for intonation including both "E" Major and "c#" minor:

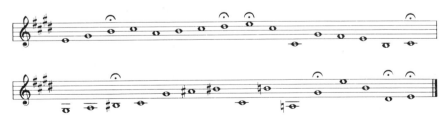

b. Form and sing the four kinds of triad in root position and inversions starting from the same note:

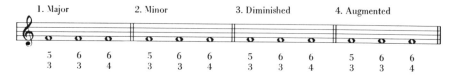

c. Recognition of triads in root position and inversions in different registers as played by the instructor.

Rhythmic Exercises

Solfège

Dictation 24

Lesson 25

1. Scales of "A♭" Major and "f" minor
2. Twelve-Beat Measures: $\frac{12}{4}$, $\frac{12}{8}$, $\frac{12}{16}$

1. "A♭" MAJOR and "f" MINOR are relative scales, inasmuch as they share the same key signature and use the same tones.

Scale of "A♭" Major

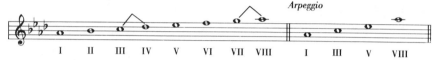

The semitones are between the III and IV and the VII and VIII steps.

Scale of "f" minor

—the ***natural*** "f" minor has semitones between the II and III and the V and VI steps.

—the ***harmonic*** "f" minor has semitones between the II and III, the V and VI, and the VII and VIII steps.

—the ***melodic*** "f" minor has semitones upward between the II and III and the VII and VIII steps, and downward between the VI and V and the III and II steps.

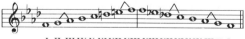

2. Compound TWELVE-BEAT MEASURES are based on four ternary meters. Because the four simple meters are joined together, there are four accents, periodically repeated in each measure:

—the ***main accent*** on the first beat

—the ***secondary accents*** on the fourth, seventh, and tenth beats.

Ex. 57

The conducting patterns are:
    fast or moderate tempo   slow tempo

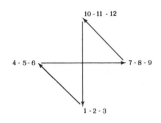
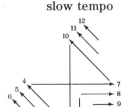

Ear-Training Exercises

    a. Exercise for intonation including both "A♭" Major and "f" minor:

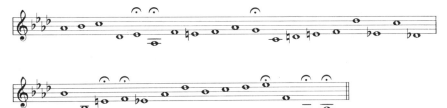

b. Build up and sing the four kinds of triad in root position and inversions starting on the same note:

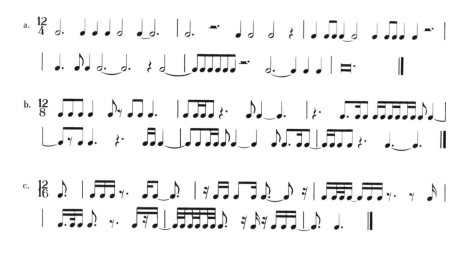

	1. Major			2. Minor			3. Diminished			4. Augmented		
	5	6	6	5	6	6	5	6	6	5	6	6
	3	3	4	3	3	4	3	3	4	3	3	4

c. Exercise for recognition of triads in root position and inversions in different registers as played by the instructor.

Rhythmic Exercises

Solfège

Dictation 25

Lesson 26

1. Scales of "B" Major and "g#" minor
2. Double Accidentals

1. "B" MAJOR and "g#" MINOR are relative scales. They have the same key signature and use the same tones.

Scale of "B" Major

The semitones are between the III and IV and the VII and VIII steps.

Scale of "g#" minor

—the **natural** "g#" minor with semitones between the II and III and the V and VI steps.

—the **harmonic** "g#" minor with semitones between the II and III, V and VI, and VII and VIII steps.

—the **melodic** "g#" minor with semitones upward between the II and III and the VII and VIII steps, and downward between the VI and V and the III and II steps.

2. DOUBLE ACCIDENTALS modify the pitch of the tones by two semitones:

—**double sharp,**   [X] —raises by two semitones
—**double flat,**   [♭♭] —lowers by two semitones

Ex. 58

Ear-Training Exercises

a. Exercise for intonation including both "B" Major and "g#" minor:

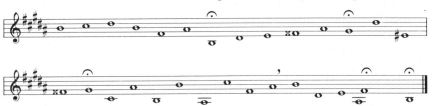

b. Build up and sing the four kinds of triad in root position and inversions starting on the same note:

1. Major			2. Minor			3. Diminished			4. Augmented		
5	6	6	5	6	6	5	6	6	5	6	6
3	3	4	3	3	4	3	3	4	3	3	4

c. Review for recognition of triads in root position and inversions in different registers as played by the instructor.

Rhythmic Exercises

New rhythmic formula:

NOTE: This rhythmic formula is used as a basic pattern for the Merenque, a Spanish dance with a sensual character, in double time and moderate tempo.

Ex. 59

Solfège

Dictation 26

Lesson 27

1. Scales of "D♭" Major and "b♭" minor
2. Generalities about the Seventh Chords: The Dominant Seventh Chord

1. "D♭" MAJOR and "b♭" MINOR or relative scales. Both have the same key signature and use the same tones.

Scale of "D♭" Major

The semitones are between the III and IV and the VII and VIII steps.

Scale of "b♭" minor

—the *natural* "b♭" minor has semitones between the II and III and the V and VI steps.

—the *harmonic* "b♭" minor has semitones between the II and III, the V and VI, and the VII and VIII steps.

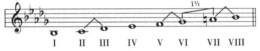

—the *melodic* "b♭" minor has semitones upward between the II and III and the VII and VIII steps, and downward between the VI and V and the III and II steps.

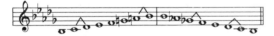

2. The SEVENTH CHORD is the simultaneous sounding of four tones superimposed at intervals of thirds.

• The DOMINANT SEVENTH CHORD (V₇) can be found on the V step of the Major or harmonic minor scales and includes the following *elements:*

C Major or:
c minor: V^7

Depending on which element is the lowest (or base) note, the V_7 chord occurs in the root position and three inversions.

Ex. 60

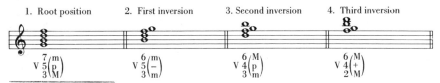

1. Root position   2. First inversion   3. Second inversion   4. Third inversion

$$V\,{5}{7}{3}\binom{m}{p}{M}\qquad V\,{5}{6}{3}\binom{m}{-}{m}\qquad V\,{4}{6}{3}\binom{M}{p}{m}\qquad V\,{4}{6}{2}\binom{M}{+}{M}$$

NOTE: Different types of Seventh Chords are presented in Lessons 35, 40, and 41.

Ear-Training Exercises

a. Exercise for intonation including both "D♭" Major and "b♭" minor:

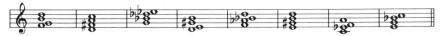

b. Form and sing the V_7 chord in root position and inversions on the following notes:

c. Exercise for recognition of V_7 chords in root position and inversions played by the instructor:

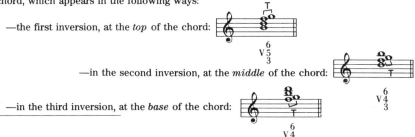

NOTE: For aural recognition of the V_7 chord in inversions, check the *whole-tone* distance of the chord, which appears in the following ways:

—the first inversion, at the *top* of the chord:

$$V\,{5}{6}{3}$$

—in the second inversion, at the *middle* of the chord:

$$V\,{4}{6}{3}$$

—in the third inversion, at the *base* of the chord:

$$V\,{4}{6}{2}$$

Rhythmic Exercises

Solfège

Dictation 27

Lesson 28

1. Scales of "F#" Major and "d#" minor
2. The Sextuplet

1. "F#" MAJOR and "d#" MINOR are relative scales. They share a common key signature and use the same tones.

Scale of "F#" Major

The semitones are between the III and IV and the VII and VIII steps.

Scale of "d#" minor

—the **natural** "d#" minor has semitones between the II and III and the V and VI steps.

—the **harmonic** "d#" minor has semitones between the II and III, the V and VI, and the VII and VIII steps.

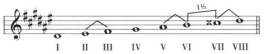

—the **melodic** "d#" minor has semitones upward between the II and III and the VII and VIII steps, and downward between the VI and V and the III and II steps.

2. The SEXTUPLET is a group of six equal notes performed in the time allotted to four of the same value. For a clear graphical representation, write the number 6 along with either the legato or bracket above or below the formula.

Ex. 61

The sextuplet can appear in three different guises, depending on the number of accents:

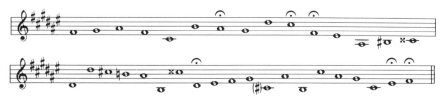

(double-triplet)

Ear-Training Exercises

a. Exercise for intonation including "F#" Major and "d#" minor:

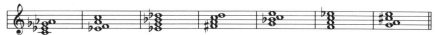

b. Form and sing the V_7 chord in root position and inversions on the following notes:

c. Sing and identify the root position and inversions of the following V_7 chords:

d. Exercise for recognition of V_7 chords in root position and inversions played by the instructor:

Rhythmic Exercises

Solfège

103.

Dictation 28

Lesson 29

1. Scales of "G♭" Major and "e♭" minor

$$5 \quad 5 \quad 5$$
2. The Five-Beat Measures: 4, 8, 16

1. Because they share the same key signature and employ the same tones, "G♭" MAJOR and "e♭" MINOR are relative scales.

Scale of "G♭" Major

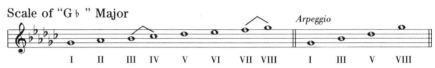

I   II   III   IV   V   VI   VII   VIII   I   III   V   VIII

The semitones are between the III and IV and the VII and VIII steps.

Scale of "e♭" minor

—the ***natural*** "e♭" minor with semitones between the II and III and the V and VI steps.

I   II III   IV   V VI VII VIII   I   III   V VIII

—the ***harmonic*** "e♭" minor with semitones between the II and III, V and VI, and VII and VIII steps.

I   II   III   IV   V   VI   VII   VIII

—the ***melodic*** "e♭" minor with semitones upward between the II and III and the VII and VIII steps, and downward between the VI and V and the III and II steps.

I II III IV V VI VII VIII VIII VII VI V IV III II I

2. The compound FIVE-BEAT MEASURES consist of an interchangeable double and triple meter.

There are two accents in this kind of measure:

—the *main accent* is always on the first beat and is repeated periodically in each measure

—the *secondary accent* occurs on the third or fourth beat depending which succession of simple meters is applied.

The five-beat measures are:

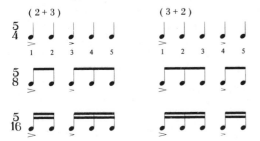

The conducting patterns are:

a. fast or moderate tempo

b. slow tempo

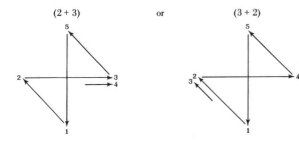

Ear-Training Exercises

a. Exercise for intonation including "Gb" Major and "eb" minor:

b. Combine the exercise below: Form and sing V₇ chords in root position and inversions on the same note:

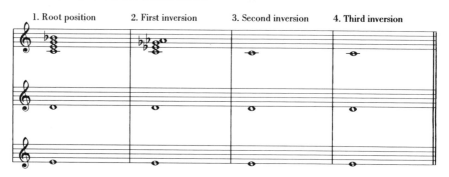

c. Exercise for recognition of V₇ chords in root position and inversions played by the instructor:

Rhythmic Exercises

Solfège

Dictation 29

Lesson 30

1. Scales of "C#" Major and "a#" minor

2. The Seven-Beat Measures: $\overset{7}{4}, \overset{7}{8}, \overset{7}{16}$

1. "C#" MAJOR and "a#" MINOR are relative scales. They have the same key signature and component tones.

Scale of "C#" Major

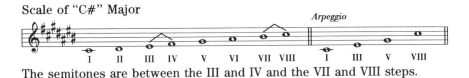

The semitones are between the III and IV and the VII and VIII steps.

Scale of "a#" minor

—the **natural** "a#" minor has semitones between the II and III and the V and VI steps.

—the **harmonic** "a#" minor has semitones between the II and III, the V and VI and the VII and VIII steps.

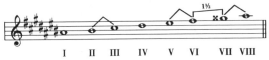

—the **melodic** "a#" minor has semitones upward between the II and III and the VII and VIII steps and downward between the VI and V and the III and II steps.

2. The compound SEVEN-BEAT MEASURES consist of one triple and two double meters. There are three accents:

—the ***main accent*** on the first beat which is repeated periodically in each measure

—the ***secondary accents*** which occur on different beats, depending on the succession of the simple meters.

The seven-beat measures are

The conducting patterns for seven beat measures are:
  a. fast or moderate tempo

(3 + 2 + 2)   (2 + 3 + 2)   (2 + 2 + 3)

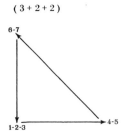

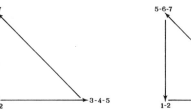
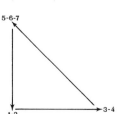

  b. slow tempo

    (3 + 2 + 2)   (2 + 3 + 2)   (2 + 2 + 3)

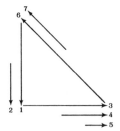
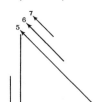

Ear-Training Exercises

a. Exercise for intonation including "C#" Major and "a#" minor:

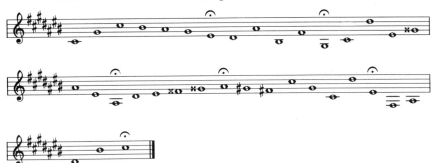

b. Review of Intervals:

1. Form and sing the simple intervals—Major, minor, augmented and diminished—on the notes below:

2. Starting from the base note, construct and sing the inversion of the following intervals:

3. Form and sing all the compound intervals on the tones suggested below:

4. Exercise for recognition of simple and compound intervals in all registers as played by the instructor.

Rhythmic Exercises

(3 + 2 + 2)

Dictation 30

Lesson 31

1. Scales of "C♭" Major and "a♭" minor
2. Variants of the Major Scale

1. "C♭" MAJOR and "a♭" MINOR are relative scales, inasmuch as both have the same key signature and use the same tones.

Scale of "C♭" Major

The semitones are between the III and IV and the VII and VIII steps.

Scale of "a♭" minor

—the ***natural*** "a♭" minor with semitones between the II and III and the V and VI steps.

—the ***harmonic*** "a♭" minor with semitones between the II and III, the V and VI, and the VII and VIII steps.

—the ***melodic*** "a♭" minor with semitones upward, between the II and III and the VII and VIII steps, and downward between the VI and V and the III and II steps.

NOTE: for a brief presentation of the scales discussed previously, see the Table of Major and Minor Diatonic Scales, p. 131.

2. VARIANTS OF THE MAJOR SCALE are obtained by lowering various degrees of the natural scale.

Variants of "C" Major scale

● NATURAL "C" Major has semitones between the III and IV and the VII and VIII steps.

● HARMONIC "C" Major is obtained by lowering the VI step by one semitone, thus obtaining a sequence of three semitones between the III and IV, the V and VI, and the VII and VIII steps. The characteristic interval of this scale is the 1-1/2 step distance or *augmented second* between the VI and VII steps.

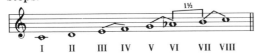

● MELODIC "C" Major is obtained by lowering the VI and VII steps one semitone. These alterations remain the same upward and downward. There are two semitones between the III and IV and the V and VI steps.

NOTE:—The altered notes which belong to the harmonic or melodic C Major can also be found in its parallel minor scale, c minor.

—In Western music, the natural form is the most frequently used of the three Major-scale variants. The harmonic and melodic scales appear most frequently in the music of the Balkans, the Middle East, and the Far East—notably India.

Ear-Training Exercises

a. Exercise for intonation including "C♭" Major and "a♭" minor:

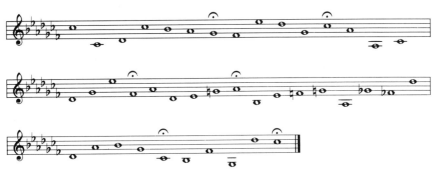

b. Form and sing the three variants of the following Major scales: G, F, B.

c. Review of the Chords:

1. Build up and sing the four kinds of triad in root position and inversions on the same note:

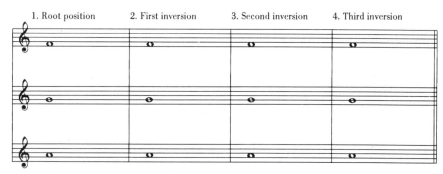

2. Form and sing V₇ chords in root position and inversions starting on the same note:

3. Exercise for recognition of triads and V₇ chords in root position and inversions in different registers as played by the instructor.

Rhythmic Exercises

Solfège

NOTE: Solfèges 112 and 113 are based on variants of Major scales and also include chromatic elements.

Dictation 31

Table of Major and Minor Diatonic Scales

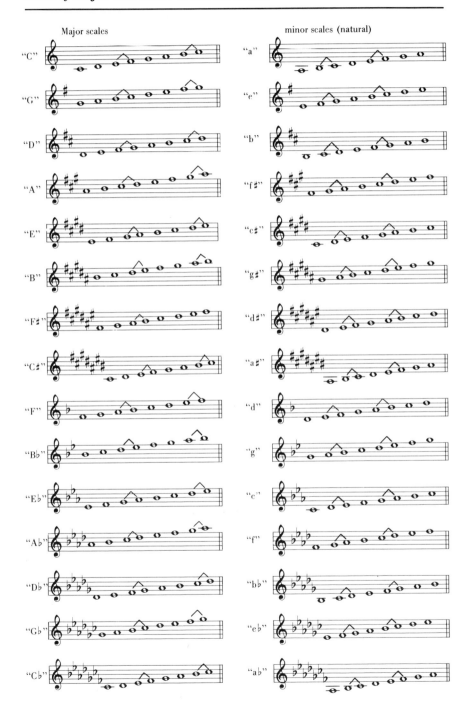

Major scales   minor scales (natural)

PART TWO
The Chromatic System

Lesson 32

1. Diatonic and Chromatic Semitones
2. Closely Related Keys
3. The Tonal Chromaticization of the Major Scale

1. The whole tone includes two semitones. The semitones are of two kinds:

- DIATONIC SEMITONE—occurs between two steps of different names.

Ex. 62 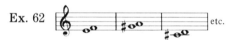 etc.

- CHROMATIC SEMITONE—occurs on the same step by use of alterations.

Ex. 63 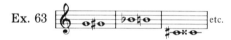 etc.

NOTE: It has been scientifically determined that a whole tone interval consists of nine *commas* (Gk.-komma) which are smaller intervals than the semitone. The diatonic semitone includes four commas, while the chromatic semitone has five commas. The inclusion of both kinds of semitones in one tone gives a total of nine commas.

Ex. 64

---

2. CLOSELY RELATED KEYS have the same key signature or differ by no more than one sharp or flat. Because of this, the related keys have most of their notes in common.
For a Major scale, the closely related keys are
—its relative minor
—key of the dominant and its relative minor
—key of the subdominant and its relative minor

Ex. 65 Closely related keys of "C" Major:

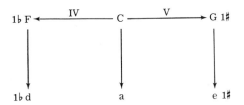

3. There are two possibilities for forming chromatic scales:
- TONAL CHROMATICIZATION—an alteration of a scale which respects the closely related keys of the main key.
- ATONAL CHROMATICIZATION—an alteration of a scale which does not respect the key relationship. (See Lesson 34.)

For TONAL CHROMATICIZATION OF A MAJOR SCALE, the following rules are applied:

—upward, the steps are ascendingly altered except for the VI step, which remains the same while the VII step is lowered.

—downward, the steps are descendingly altered except for the V step, which remains the same while the IV step is raised.

The process of chromaticization produces twelve semitones: *diatonic* between the III and IV and the VII and VIII steps, and *chromatic* between all others.

All the chromatic elements obtained in this process belong to one of the closely related keys and their variants.

Ex. 66

The chromatic "C" Major.

NOTE: For reference to the three variants of Major scales, see Lesson 31.

Ear-Training Exercises

a. Form and sing the diatonic and chromatic semitones on the following tones:

b. Exercise for intonation using the chromatic "C" Major:

c. Form and sing the chromatic Major scales on the tones suggested below:

d. On the first note given below, identify the tones of a short chromatic passage played by the instructor:

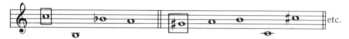

Rhythmic Exercises

a. [rhythmic notation in 2/4 time]

b. [rhythmic notation in 3/4 time]

Solfège

Dictation 32

Lesson 33

1. Closely related keys (continued)
2. The Tonal Chromaticization of the Minor Scale

1. The CLOSELY RELATED KEYS of a minor key are
—its relative Major
—key of the dominant and its relative Major
—key of the subdominant and its relative Major

Ex. 67 Closely related keys of "a" minor:

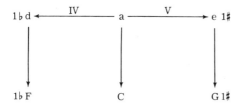

2. The TONAL CHROMATICIZATION OF THE MINOR SCALE respects the key relationship. All the chromatic elements obtained in this process belong to the closely related keys and their variants. The following rules are applied to form chromatic minor scales:

—upward, the steps are ascendingly altered except for the I step, which remains the same while the II step is lowered.

—downward, there are two possibilities: use the technique of the above upward process; or descendingly alter the V, IV, and II steps, which produces the same notes as its relative chromatic Major scale.

Ex. 68 Chromatic "a" minor:

Ear-Training Exercises

a. Form and sing the diatonic and chromatic semitones on these suggested tones:

b. Exercise for intonation based on the chromatic "a" minor:

c. Build up and sing chromatic minor scales on the following tones:

d. On the first note given below, name the notes of a short chromatic passage played by the instructor:

Rhythmic Exercises

Solfège

Dictation 33

Lesson 34

1. Atonal Chromaticization
2. Enharmonics

1. The ATONAL CHROMATICIZATION of the Major and minor scales is not based on key relationship. The rules applied in this process are that upward, the steps are ascendingly altered, and downward, they are descendingly altered.

Ex. 69

The chromatic "C" Major

| | I | | II | | III | IV | | V | | VI | | VII | VIII | VIII | VII | | VI | | V | | IV | III | | II | | I |

The chromatic "a" minor

| | I | | II | III | | IV | | V | VI | | VII | | VIII | VIII | | VII | | VI | V | | IV | | III | II | | I |

2. ENHARMONICS are different spellings of the same tone, interval, or key.
* ENHARMONIC TONES—have the same pitch but different names.

Ex. 70

etc.

* ENHARMONIC INTERVALS—sound alike but have different quantity and quality.

Ex. 71

etc.

4+ = 5–   3M = 4–

- ENHARMONIC KEYS—have different key signatures, and use notes of the same pitch which have different names.

Ex. 72

NOTE:—Enharmonism is marked by the sign [=]

  —It should be mentioned that the principle of "equal temperament" divides the octave into twelve equal semitones. In this system, enharmonic tones have the same pitch, while in the "mean-tone" system there is a difference of almost a quarter-tone between enharmonic tones. For more information, see W. Apel, *Harvard Dictionary of Music*, "Temperament."

Ear-Training Exercises

  a. Form and sing chromatic Major and minor scales on the notes mentioned below, using atonal chromaticization:

  b. Exercise for intonation in chromatic "a" minor, including enharmonic tones:

  c. Form and sing the enharmonic intervals of the suggested examples below:

  d. On the first note given below, identify the tones of a short chromatic passage played by the instructor:

etc.

Rhythmic Exercises

Solfège

Dictation 34

Lesson 35

1. Modulation
2. The Diminished Seventh Chord

1. MODULATION is a change of key within a composition. In harmony, modulation is accomplished by the use of 'pivot' chord; that is, simply a chord which is related to both the initial and the new key. Although the exercises in this book are written for one part only, harmonic implications within a given piece should be noticed.

Generally there are three different stages in the process of modulation:

—establishment of the initial key
—proper modulation by the use of a pivot chord
—establishment of the new key

NOTE: Beginning with the music of the late 19th century, the method mentioned above is not always applied in musical composition. Many times abrupt modulation, or the technique of continuous modulation—mainly developed by Wagner—lacks one of the three stages.

There are three kinds of modulation:

• DIATONIC MODULATION—occurs chiefly between closely related keys and is accomplished by the use of a pivot chord that is diatonic in both keys.

Ex. 73 From C Major to a minor (harmonic)

• CHROMATIC MODULATION—occurs between both closely related and remote keys and is accomplished by the use of a pivot chord that is chromatic in one or both keys.

Ex. 74 From E♭ Major to d minor (harmonic)

- ENHARMONIC MODULATION—occurs between remote keys and is accomplished by the use of a pivot chord of which one or more notes are enharmonically changed.

Ex. 75 from C Major to c# minor (melodic)

NOTE: The abbreviation d_7 refers to the diminished seventh chord. See Lesson 35/2.

2. The DIMINISHED SEVENTH CHORD is the simultaneous sounding of four tones superimposed at minor third intervals, which causes a similar sonorous effect in the root position and its inversions.

This type of chord in the root position includes the diminished fifth and seventh intervals, and can generally be found on the VII degree of the harmonic minor scale.

Ex. 76

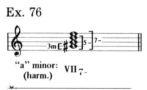

NOTE: The diminished seventh chord also occurs in major and minor scales on chromatically altered steps. See Ex. 75, above.

Ear-Training Exercises

a. Exercise for intonation including the diatonic, chromatic, and enharmonic modulation:

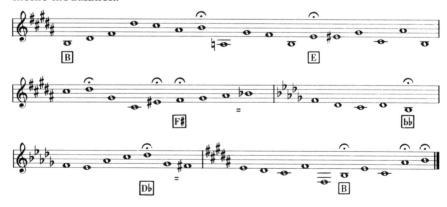

b. Form and sing diminished seventh chords in root position on the following tones:

c. Build up and sing diminished seventh chords on the notes suggested by the instructor.

Rhythmic Exercises

New rhythmic formula:

(rhythmic notation)

(rhythmic exercises a. and b. in musical notation)

Solfège

Moderato risoluto M.M. ♩ = 78

124.

Dictation 35

PART THREE
The Modal System

Lesson 36

1. Pentatonic Scale: Anhemitonic
2. The Eight-Beat Measures: 8   8
                             8   16

1. PENTATONIC SCALE is a succession of five steps build on second and third intervals.

- The ANHEMITONIC PENTATONIC SCALE consists of successive Major 2nd and minor 3rd intervals.

Ex. 77

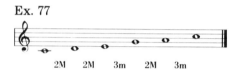

NOTE: Anhemitonic (Gk.: an = without; hemi = half; tonos = tones)—without semitones.
Hemitonic—with semitones.

Using the same notes and starting from different steps, the following positions of th pentatonic scale are produced:

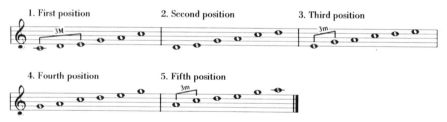

Comparing these different positions, the scale is:

—Major mode in the first position because of the Major 3rd interval between the I and III steps

—minor mode in the third and fifth positions because of the minor 3rd interval between the I and II steps

—neutral in the second and fourth positions because of the exclusion of the 3rd interval, which would determine the mode.

The utilization of pentatonic scales is common, particularly in the music of the Balkans, Japan, China, and various regions of Africa.

2. The compound EIGHT-BEAT MEASURES are based on irregular or mixed meters: two of three beats, and one of two beats. In these kinds of measure, there are three successive accents:

—the **main accent** on the first beat, which is periodically repeated

—the **secondary accents** on various beats, depending on the succession of simple meters.

The following eight-beat measures are commonly used:

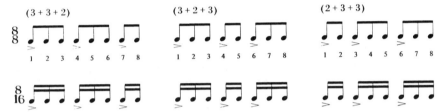

The conducting patterns are:

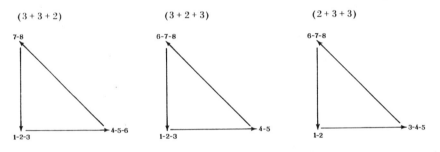

Ear-Training Exercises

a. Build up and sing the anhemitonic pentatonic scales in all positions on the following tones:

b. Sing and determine the positions of the pentatonic scales below:

c. Form and sing the anhemitonic pentatonic scales on the notes indicated by the instructor.

Rhythmic Exercises

Solfège

Dictation 36

Lesson 37

1. Pentatonic Scale: Hemitonic
2. Abbreviations

1. The HEMITONIC PENTATONIC SCALE is based on the succession of Major and minor 2nd, and Major 3rd intevals.

Ex. 78

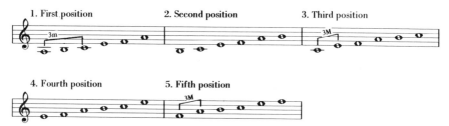

The positions of this scale are

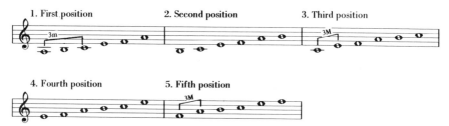

As a result of the positions above, the scale is
—minor mode in the first position, because of the minor 3rd interval between the I and III steps.
—Major mode in the third and fifth positions because of the Major 3rd interval between the I and II steps.
—neutral in the second and fourth positions because of the exclusion of the 3rd interval, which would determine the mode.

NOTE: The so-called "pien" or passing tones [●] are those which are not included in the basic pentatonic scale.

Ex. 79

---

2. ABBREVIATIONS, which can be either signs or terms, simplify the writing of music:

—repetition of fragments:

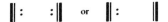

—repetition of measures, rhythmic figures, and tones:

—tremolo on the same or alternating notes:

—for rests of several measures is used:

—terms:

da capo (D.C.) = from the beginning
da capo al fine (D.C. al fine) = from the beginning to *fine*
dal segno ⅹ *al fine* = from the sign ⅹ to *fine*

con 8-va alta = with the higher octave;

Ex. 80

con 8-va bassa = with the lower octave;

Ex. 81

Ear-Training Exercises

a. Form and sing all the positions of the hemitonic pentatonic scale on the following notes:

b. Sing and identify the positions of the pentatonic scales below:

c. Build up and sing the hemitonic pentatonic scales on the tones indicated by the instructor.

Rhythmic Exercises

Solfège

Dictation 37

Lesson 38

1. Medieval Modes: Ionian, Dorian
2. Ornaments

1. MEDIEVAL MODES, or church modes, are the result of a long historical process crystallized in the sixteenth century. The names of these modes,
borrowed from ancient Greek modes and applied to entirely different
structures, are used to designate eight church modes: four *authentic*
modes—the Dorian, Phrygian, Lydian, and Mixolydian—and four derived
plagals.

NOTE: The four authentic modes and their plagals are:

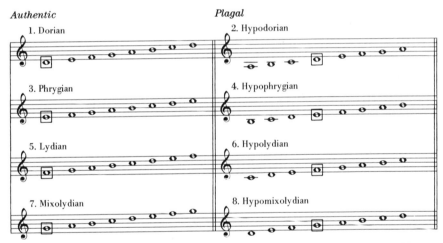

Authentic
1. Dorian
3. Phrygian
5. Lydian
7. Mixolydian

Plagal
2. Hypodorian
4. Hypophrygian
6. Hypolydian
8. Hypomixolydian

The most important tone of the mode is the so-called *vox finalis* (Lat.) marked by ☐

Two other authentic modes, the Ionian and Aeolian along with their
plagals, were described by Glareanus in *Dodecachordon* (1547). The
Hyperaeolian and Hyperphrygian modes, also mentioned in this work, became the Locrian mode and its plagal.

Because of the similarities among various authentic and plagal modes, the
process of eliminating the plagals was begun in the late sixteenth century,
and gradually musical practice concentrated on the seven authentic modes:
the Ionian, Dorian, Phrygian, Lydian, Mixolydian, Aeolian, and Locrian.

For this reason, only the above seven modes will be presented in the
following lessons.

- The IONIAN mode is similar to a Major scale but does not emphasize the tonal attractions between the Tonic, Subdominant, and Dominant degrees of the diatonic scale. The semitones of this mode are between the III and IV and the VII and VIII steps. Intervals formed on the I step are the Major 3rd, 6th, and 7th.

Ex. 82

The Ionian mode on "c"

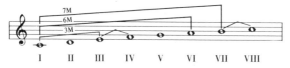

NOTE: A common way to determine the structure of the modes is to examine the relationship of the III, VI, and VII steps to the I step.

- The DORIAN mode has semitones between the II and III and the VI and VII steps. Intervals formed on the I step are the minor 3rd, the Major, or *Dorian, sixth,* and the minor 7th.

Ex. 83

Dorian mode on "d"

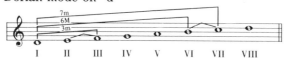

The Dorian mode can be found on the II step of any Major scale. Because of this, a recommended method of determining the key signature of any Dorian mode is to count a descending Major 2nd interval from the first step of the mode.

Ex. 84

The Dorian mode on "a" has the key signature of "G" Major.

2. ORNAMENTS, which can be indicated by either signs or letters, are used for the purpose of enriching the melody of a musical composition. Practiced widely in the music of the sixteenth century, ornamentation was generally improvised. Later, in the seventeenth century, the French harpsichordists developed a system of performing ornaments, a system that is still used today:

• APPOGGIATURA—a note or a group of notes that temporarily displaces the principal or main note of a melody. Multiple forms are used in practice:

—short:

simple [♪♩]   double [♫♩]   triple [♫♩]

—long [♪♩]

Ex. 85

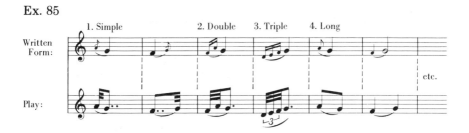

• MORDENT—a fast alternation between the main note and the immediate upper or lower note. There are various forms such as

—simple:
    upper [∿];
    lower [∿];
—double:
    upper [∿∿];
    lower [∿∿];

Ex. 86

• TURN—a group of notes in which the alternation between the upper, main, and lower notes is indicated by signs:

—upper [∞]
—lower [∞]

Ex. 87

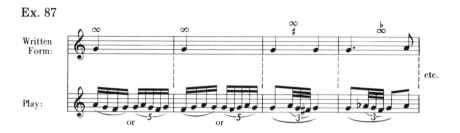

• TRILL [*tr* or ⌇⌇⌇]—a fast alternation between the main note and its immediate upper neighbor.

Ex. 88

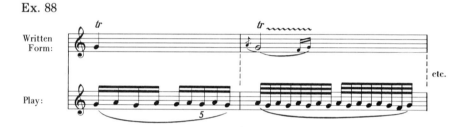

• ARPEGGIO [ ]—a broken chord that consists of successively playing the notes of the chord.

Ex. 89

• GLISSANDO [ ]—a sliding from one note to another by playing or singing all the notes included in between.

NOTE: In performing ornaments, it is important to consider the style of composition. For example, the "old trill" of Baroque instrumental music, which is supposed to be performed not "as fast as possible," contrasts with the increased speed of the nineteenth century trill.

Ear-Training Exercises

a. Form and sing the Dorian mode starting on the following tones:

b. Build up and sing the Dorian modes, respecting the given key signatures below:

Ex. 90

c. Build up and sing the Dorian mode on the notes given by the instructor.

Rhythmic Exercises

Solfège

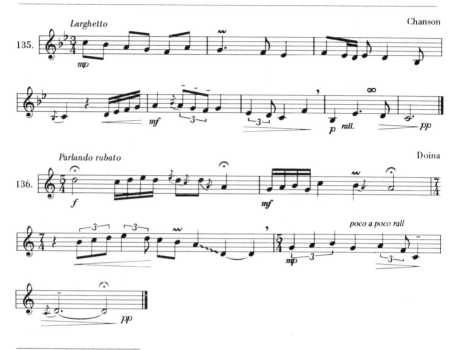

NOTE: "Doina"—a type of Romanian folk song of melancholy character, employing free rhythm and an abundance of ornament.

Dictation 38

Lesson 39

1. Medieval Modes: Phrygian, Lydian
2. The Duplet

1. • The PHRYGIAN mode is characterized by semitones between the I and II and the V and VI steps. Intervals formed on the I step are the minor 3rd, 6th, and 7th. The characteristic interval of this mode is the minor, or *Phrygian, second* between the I and II steps.

Ex. 91

Phrygian mode on "e"

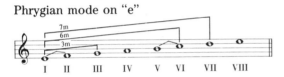

I	II	III	IV	V	VI	VII	VIII

The Phrygian mode can be found on the III step of any Major scale. To build this mode on different tones and to find its key signature, count a descending Major 3rd interval from the I step of the mode.

Ex. 92
The Phrygian mode on "a" has the key signature of "F" Major.

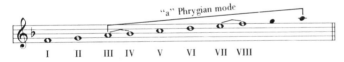

I	II	III	IV	V	VI	VII	VIII

• The LYDIAN mode has semitones between the IV and V and the VII and VIII steps. Intervals formed on the I step are the Major 3rd, 6th, and 7th. The characteristic interval of this mode is the *augmented fourth* between the I and IV steps.

Ex. 93

Lydian mode on "f"

I	II	III	IV	V	VI	VII	VIII

The Lydian mode is located on the IV step of any Major scale. To form this mode on different tones and to find its key signature, count a descending perfect 4th interval from the I step of the mode.

Ex. 94

The Lydian mode on "a" has the key signature of "E" Major.

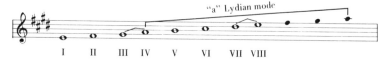

I	II	III	IV	V	VI	VII	VIII

2. The DUPLET is a group of two equal notes played in the time of three notes of the same value. The graphic representation of this rhythmic pattern includes the number 2 and either the legato or bracket above or below the formula.

Ex. 95

Ear-Training Exercises

a. Build up and sing the Phrygian and Lydian modes on the following tones:

b. Construct and sing the Phrygian and Lydian modes, respecting the key signatures given below:

c. Form and sing the Phrygian and Lydian modes on the notes suggested by the instructor.

Rhythmic Exercises

Solfège

Dictation 39

Lesson 40

1. Medieval Modes: Mixolydian, Aeolian, Locrian
2. Seventh Chords

1. • The MIXOLYDIAN mode has semitones between the III and IV and the VI and VII steps. Intervals formed on the I step are the Major 3rd, the Major 6th, and the minor 7th, which is called the *Mixolydian seventh.*

Ex. 96

Mixolydian mode on "g"

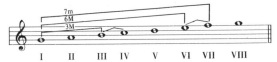

This mode can be found on the V step of any Major scale. To form the Mixolydian mode on different tones and to find its key signature, count a descending perfect 5th interval from the I step of the mode.

Ex. 97

The Mixolydian mode on "a" has the key signature of "D" Major.

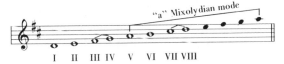

• The AEOLIAN mode is similar to the natural minor scale, but does not emphasize the tonal attractions between the Tonic, Subdominant, and Dominant degrees of the diatonic scale. The semitones are between the II and III and the V and VI steps. Intervals formed on the I step of this mode are the minor 3rd, 6th, and 7th.

Ex. 98

Aeolian mode on "a"

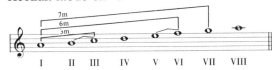

• The LOCRIAN mode has semitones between the I and II and the IV and V steps. Intervals formed on the I step are the minor 3rd, 6th, and 7th. This mode is less used than the modes previously mentioned because of its instability, which is a result of the diminished 5th interval, or *Locrian fifth,* included between the I and V steps.

Ex. 99

Locrian mode on "b"

I   II   III   IV   V   VI   VII   VIII

The Locrian mode is located on the VII step of any Major scale. To form this mode on different tones and to identify its key signature, count an ascending minor 2nd interval from the mode's first step.

Ex. 100

The Locrian mode on "a" has the key signature of "Bb" Major:

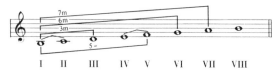

I   II   III IV   V   VI VII VIII

2. SEVENTH CHORDS result from various combinations between the four kinds of triad and 7th intervals. These chords can be obtained by
—adding a Major or minor 7th interval to the Major triad.

Ex. 101

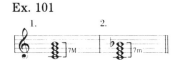

—adding a Major or minor 7th interval to the minor triad.

Ex. 102

NOTE: The Major triad with the minor 7th is called the "Dominant seventh chord." (See Lesson 27.)

Ear-Training Exercises

a. Starting on the following tones, form and sing the Mixolydian, Aeolian, and Locrian modes:

b. Build up and sing these three modes, respecting the given key signatures:

1. Mixolydian modes   2. Aeolian modes   3. Locrian modes

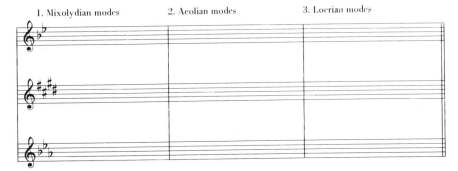

c. Form and sing the seventh chords obtained by combinations of Major or minor triad and 7th intervals on the following tones:

d. Identify by ear the structure of the following seventh chords played by the instructor:

Rhythmic Exercises

Solfège

Dictation 40

Lesson 41

1. Chromatic Modes: Ionian
2. Seventh Chords (continued)

1. The CHROMATIC MODES are obtained from the diatonic or natural modes by ascending or descending alterations of various degrees. There are several kinds of chromatic mode. These are characteristic features of Oriental and Balkan music. However, only a few frequently used ones will be presented in the following lessons.

The CHROMATIC IONIAN mode usually has three different forms

—Ionian mode with raised IV, and lowered VII degree. There are two semitones between the IV and V and the VI and VII steps. Also, there are two characteristic intervals, the augmented 4th and the minor 7th on the I step of the mode.

Ex. 103

Chromatic Ionian mode on "C"

—Ionian mode with the raised II and IV, and lowered VII degree. It is interesting to observe that in this mode there is a succession of three semitones, between the II and III, the IV and V and the VI and VII steps. The characteristic intervals of this mode are the augmented 2nd and 4th, and the minor 7th on the I step.

Ex. 104

Chromatic Ionian mode on "c"

—Ionian mode with both a lowered II and VI degree. This is one of the most interesting modes and includes four semitones, between the I and II, III and IV, V and VI, and VII and VIII steps. There are two augmented 2nd intervals, between the II and III and the VI and VII steps, giving this mode the name of ***double harmonic.***

Ex. 105

Chromatic Ionian mode on "c"

I   II   III IV   V   VI   VII VIII

2. In addition to the SEVENTH CHORDS mentioned in Lesson 40, two other chords are currently used in musical practice, as a result of the simultaneous sounding of triads and 7th intervals. These chords are obtained by:

—adding a Major, minor, or diminished 7th interval to the diminished triad

Ex. 106

—adding a Major or minor 7th interval to the augmented triad

Ex. 107

NOTE: The simultaneous sounding of the diminished triad and the diminished 7th interval has previously been referred to as the ***diminished seventh chord.*** (See Lesson 35.)

Ear-Training Exercises

a. Exercise for intonation including various elements of the chromatic Ionian mode:

b. Build up and sing the chromatic Ionian modes on the notes suggested below:

c. Form and sing the seventh chords which result from combinations of augmented and diminished triads and 7th intervals on the following notes:

d. Exercise for recognition of seventh chords played by the instructor:

Rhythmic Exercises

New rhythmic formulas for the development of syncopation:

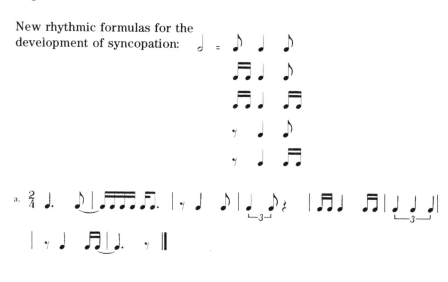

Solfège

Dictation 41

Lesson 42

1. Chromatic Modes: Lydian, Mixolydian
2. Ninth Chords

1. • The CHROMATIC LYDIAN mode is obtained by raising the II degree of the natural mode. The semitones are between the II and III, the IV and V, and the VII and VIII steps. The characteristic intervals are the augmented 2nd and 4th, both formed on the I step of the mode.

Ex. 108

Chromatic Lydian mode on "f"

I   II III   IV V   VI   VII VIII

• The CHROMATIC MIXOLYDIAN mode can be obtained by:

—raising the II step of the natural mode, resulting in semitones between the II and III, the III and IV, and the VI and VII steps. There are two characteristic intervals on the I step—the augmented 2nd and the minor 7th.

Ex. 109

Chromatic Mixolydian mode on "g"

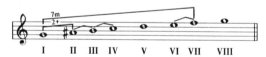

I   II   III IV   V   VI VII   VIII

—lowering the II step of the natural mode, resulting in three semitones, between the I and II, the III and IV, and the VI and VII steps. The characteristic intervals of this mode are the augmented 2nd between the II and III steps, and the minor 7th on the I step.

Ex. 110

Chromatic Mixolydian mode on "g"

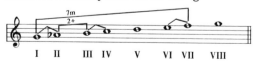

I   II   III IV   V   VI VII   VIII

2. The NINTH CHORDS consist of the simultaneous sounding of five tones superimposed at intervals of thirds. These chords can also be considered as *polychords,* or multiple chords, because of the simultaneous sounding of two superimposed triads (Major, minor, diminished, or augmented) connected by a common note. There are several combinations of triads resulting in multiple ninth chords that are used a good deal in contemporary music.

Ex. 111

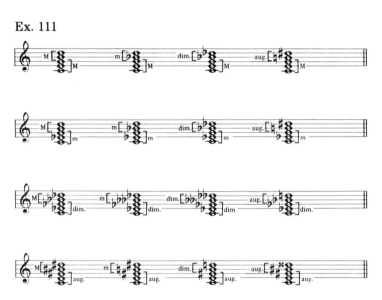

NOTE: For practice in hearing the superimposed pitch tones of the ninth chords, start from the base note and sing all the examples above.

Ear-Training Exercises

a. Exercises for intonation.
Chromatic Lydian mode with raised II degree:

Chromatic Mixolydian mode using both raised and lowered II degree:

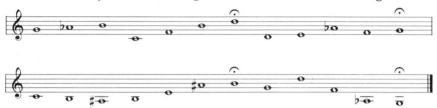

b. Form and sing the chromatic Lydian and Mixolydian modes on the notes below:

c. Starting from the base note, form and sing the previously mentioned ninth chords on the following tones:

d. Sing and identify the quality of triads included in the following ninth chords played by the instructor:

   etc.

Rhythmic Exercises

New rhythmic formula:

Solfège

Dictation 42

Lesson 43

1. Whole-Tone Scale
2. Eleventh Chords

1. The WHOLE-TONE SCALE represents one of the bases of a new orientation in late nineteenth-century music, started and extensively used by Debussy and his contemporaries.

Constructed only on whole-tone distances, this type of scale is **nonfunctional.** Tonal feeling is excluded by the absence of the Tonic-Subdominant-Dominant functions.

General rules for forming whole-tone scales on different tones are

—upward, a succession of whole-tone distances is constructed by using ascending alterations.

—downward, the tones are descendingly altered except for the III, II, and I steps, which remain the same as in the upward succession.

Ex. 112

Whole-tone scale on "C"

I   II   III   IV   V   VI   VII   VII   VI   V   IV   III   II   I

The whole-tone scale is based on the atonal chromaticization of a Major scale. (See Lesson 34.)

All the elements obtained in the scale above result from the atonal chromaticization of "C" Major by the selection of every second element going upward starting on C# in the ascending octave, then going downward, selecting every second element starting on "B".

Ex. 113

Atonal chromatic-
ization
of "C"
Major:

Whole-tone
scale on
"C":

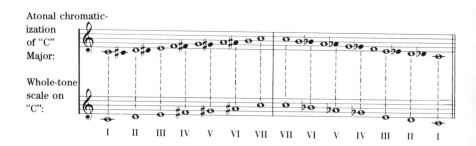

I   II   III   IV   V   VI   VII   VII   VI   V   IV   III   II   I

The foregoing process can also be started on the pitch "C#" and will result in a new whole-tone scale. Continuing this method, all other scales will include the same pitch tones as the whole-tone scales started on "C" or "C#".

One of the interesting aspects of the whole-tone scale is that the chords constructed on its degrees are all augmented.

Ex. 114

    I   II   III   IV   V   VI

NOTE: The whole-tone scale is called the **hexatonal scale** (*Gk; hexa* = six; *tonos* = tone)—six tones.

2. The ELEVENTH CHORDS consist of the simultaneous sounding of six notes superimposed at intervals of thirds. These chords can be considered as polychords, or two superimposed triads, connected by an intervening Major or minor 3rd interval.

There are several possibilities in combining different triads to obtain multiple eleventh chords. Currently, the following types of eleventh chord are used:

Ear-Training Exercises

a. Exercise for intonation based on the whole-tone scale on "C":

NOTE: The symbol [·····] indicates the diminished 3rd interval and calls attention to notes which are to be reproduced as a whole-tone distance.

b. Form and sing whole-tone scales on the following tones:

c. Memorize, sing, and identify the tones of a short passage based on the whole-tone scale starting from a given note played by the instructor.

d. Build up and sing the eleventh chords starting on the notes suggested below:

e. Sing and identify the triads included in the following eleventh chords:

f. Listen and identify the structure of the eleventh chords played by the instructor.

Ex. 115

 etc.

Rhythmic Exercises

New rhythmic formula:

a.

b.

Solfège

NOTE: Solfège 151 is based on a whole tone scale starting on "b♭".

Dictation 43

Lesson 44

1. Messiaen's Modes: First, Second, Third
2. The Quintuplet

1. The theory of modes in the modern interpretation acquires a new orientation resulting in the appearance of multiple modes with entirely different structures from the ones mentioned in previous lessons. MESSIAEN'S MODES represent one of the most valuable contributions to this development.

According to Messiaen, there are seven types of mode consisting of from seven to eleven tones, which are organized into identical groups connected by a common note.

• Messiaen's FIRST MODE is similar to the whole-tone scale and includes seven tones, which are organized in six two-note groups.

Ex. 116

• Messiaen's SECOND MODE includes nine tones, which are organized in four identical groups of three notes, each constructed on successions of semitone and tone distances.

Ex. 117

• Messiaen's THIRD MODE has ten tones that are built up in three identical groups of four notes, having the succession of one tone and two semitone distances.

NOTE: Olivier Messiaen (1908—   ) French composer, held by many music authorities to be the "most versatile and interesting of the committed composers of the twentieth century" (*Twentieth Century Music*, by H.H. Stuckenschmidt, *Twentieth Century Music*, edited by McGraw-Hill Book Company. Copyright © 1969 by H.H. Stuckenschmidt. Used by permission). He is also one of the most widely acknowledged teachers of contemporary musicians. Most of the principles of his composition techniques are explained in his theoretical work, *Technique de mon language musical* (1944). Inspired by Hindu rhythms, bird song, and electronic-instrument sonorities, his compositions have made an important contribution to the development of contemporary music.

Ex. 118

NOTE: The process of forming Messiaen's modes on all twelve tones of the chromatic scale will generate modes with identical as well as new sonorous material. Because of this, these modes are also called *modes with limited transposition.* For example, the transposition of the second mode on "d♭" and "d" produces new tones. However, on "e♭," tones of the original mode are again produced.

Ex. 119

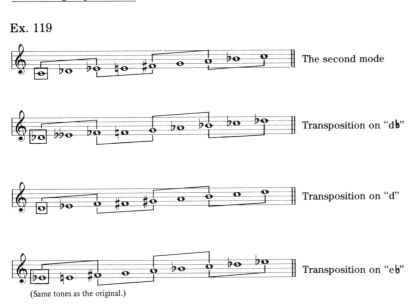

The second mode

Transposition on "d♭"

Transposition on "d"

Transposition on "e♭"

(Same tones as the original.)

2. The QUINTUPLET is a group of five equal notes played in the time allotted to four notes of the same value. It is marked by the number 5 and either the *legato* or bracket above or below the formula:

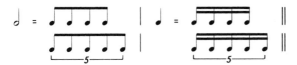

New rhythmic patterns result from joining two of the five notes from the basic formula:

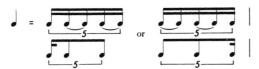

NOTE: In music theory there are two different systems for replacing a ternary or dotted note-value with a quintuplet:

—The quintuplet instead of three notes is used in German notation.
—The quintuplet instead of six notes applied in French and Italian notation.

Ex. 120

German notation:

French notation:

Ear-Training Exercises

a. Exercises for intonation based on Messiaen's second mode:

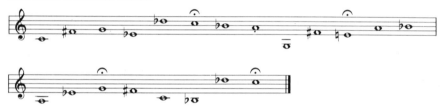

Messiaen's third mode:

NOTE: Because of the similarities between the whole-tone scale and Messiaen's first mode, see Lesson 43, Ear Training Exercises/a.

b. On the first note given below, memorize, sing, and identify the tones of a short passage based on the modes mentioned above as played by the instructor:

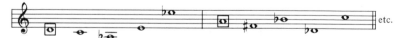

etc.

Rhythmic Exercises

a.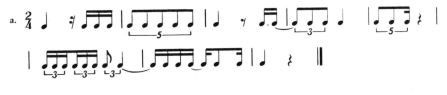

Solfège

NOTE: Solfège 153 is based on the transposition of the first Messiaen mode on "a♭."

Dictation 44

Lesson 45

1. Messiaen's Modes: Fourth, Fifth
2. Thirteenth Chords

1. • Messiaen's FOURTH MODE is based on nine successive tones organized in two identical groups of five notes, each of which includes two semitones, a one and one-half tone step, and one semitone.

Ex. 121

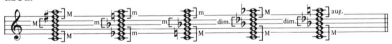

• Messiaen's FIFTH MODE includes a succession of seven tones organized in two identical groups of four notes, each of which includes a Major 3rd interval placed between two semitones.

Ex. 122

2. THIRTEENTH CHORDS are the simultaneous sounding of seven tones superimposed at intervals of thirds. These chords can also be considered as polychords consisting of the simultaneous sounding of three triads with intervening common notes. The following combinations are frequently used:

Ear-Training Exercises

a. Exercises for intonation.

Messiaen's fourth mode:

Messiaen's fifth mode:

b. Build up and sing the previously mentioned thirteenth chords on the notes suggested below:

c. Sing and identify the triads included in the following thirteenth chords:

d. Identify by ear the structure of the thirteenth chords played by the instructor in different registers.

 etc.

Rhythmic Exercises

Solfège

Dictation 45

Lesson 46

Messiaen's Modes: Sixth, Seventh

• Messiaen's SIXTH MODE consists of nine tones organized in two identical groups of five notes, each of which includes a succession of two tones and two semitones.

Ex. 123

• Messiaen's SEVENTH MODE includes eleven tones organized in two identical groups of six notes, each of which is constructed on a succession of three semitones, one tone, and one semitone.

Ex. 124

Ear-Training Exercises

NOTE: The accidentals used in the following exercises affect only the note that immediately follows.

a. Exercise for intonation.

Messiaen's sixth mode:

Messiaen's seventh mode:

b. Starting from a given note, sing and identify the tones of short passages played by the instructor based on Messiaen's sixth and seventh modes.

Ex. 125

c. *Review of the seventh, ninth, eleventh, and thirteenth chords:*
1. Build up and sing the various seventh chords which result from combinations of triads and 7th intervals on the following tones:

Triad	Intervals		
	7M	7m	7-
Major			
minor			
diminished			
augmented			

7-

2. Starting from the base note, sing and identify the structure of the following ninth chords:

3. Form and sing the eleventh chords on the notes suggested below:

4. Sing and identify the quality of triads included in the following thirteenth chords:

196

5. Identify the seventh, ninth, eleventh, and thirteenth chords in all registers as played by the instructor.

Rhythmic Exercises

Solfège

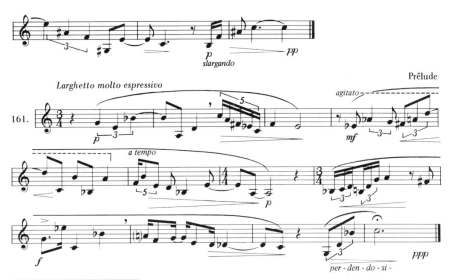

NOTE: Solfège 161 is a combination of the seventh Messiaen mode and its transposition on "d".

Dictation 46

PART FOUR
The Atonal System

Lesson 47

1. "Free" Atonality
2. The Quadruplet
3. Chords by Fourths

1. The trend of progressive negation of tonality began in late nineteenth-century music in several manifestations: continuous modulations, maximum utilization of chromaticism, nonresolution of tensions, cadence-avoiding style, and others. This trend gave rise to a new technique at the beginning of the twentieth century called ATONALISM.

Atonalism or absence of tonality represented a revolution in all aspects of musical language. Adopted first by Arnold Schönberg (works composed between 1908 and 1914) and by his followers, Anton Webern and Alban Berg, atonalism eventually became one of the frequently used techniques of contemporary music.

"FREE" ATONALITY consists of multiple combinations of the elements included in the chromatic scale with each one treated individually and with equal importance.

This technique continued to develop for almost fifteen years before being organized in the "serial" or "dodecaphonic" system. (See Lesson 48.)

2. The QUADRUPLET is a group of four equal notes, played in the same time as three notes of the same value, and represented by the number 4 and either a legato mark or a bracket, above or below the formula.

Ex. 126

3. The FOURTH CHORDS which consist of the simultaneous sounding of two or more superimposed fourth intervals are among the most frequently used chordal structures in contemporary music. Currently, the following combinations are used:

—three-note chords by fourth
Ex. 127

—four-note chords by fourth

Ex. 128

NOTE: The process of continuing superimposed fourth intervals produces fourth chords of more than four notes.

Ear-Training Exercises

To continue developing an awareness of the new features of atonal music initiated in the previous exercises based on the whole-tone scale and Messiaen's modes, increasingly complex exercises will now be introduced to allow a progressive transition away from tonality to the concept of atonality.

   a. Exercise for intonation.

NOTE: Consider all the exercises which follow as connections between intervals. Try to reproduce them internally before singing. The accidentals affect only the notes immediately following them.

1.

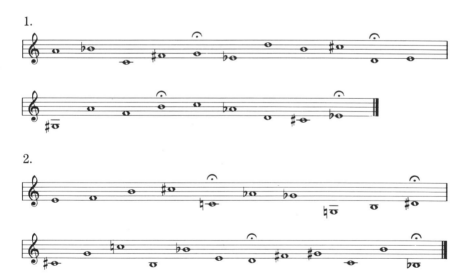

b. Starting from a given note, identify the tones of a short atonal passage played by the instructor:

c. Starting from the base note, construct and sing three-note chords by fourths on the following tones:

d. Build up and sing four-note chords by fourths on the suggested notes below:

e. Sing and identify the structure of the following fourth chords:

f. Sing and identify the structure of the fourth chords played by the instructor:

Rhythmic Exercises

Solfège

Dialogue

Dictation 47

Lesson 48

Serial Music

The new orientation in music generated by the appearance of atonality created the premise of a new system which was elaborated by Schönberg in 1923. This system, which is called the SERIAL, TWELVE-TONE, or DODECAPHONIC system, is widely used in contemporary music.

The entire process is based on well-defined techniques such as nonrepetition, perpetual variation, repetition of a group of tones in varied rhythm before the appearance of the next note of the series, and others. However, the detailed study of these devices belongs to the specialized field of analysis and composition.

Nevertheless, it is important for any musician to develop the ability *to read, hear,* and *perform* the multifarious intonational combinations that occur in the complicated rhythmic formulas frequently used in contemporary music. For this reason, a few general, but essential, explanations of the serial technique are included in this text, with related practice exercises.

- The serial technique is based on twelve preselected tones of the chromatic scale, which are organized in a SERIES or TONE ROW.
- The series is considered to have the following forms:

—the *original* [O] or basic set in the initial form

Ex. 129

—the *inversion* [I] starts from the first note of the original series which remains the same, with the direction of succeeding intervals inverted; ascending intervals become descending and vice versa

Ex. 130

—the **retrograde** [R] is the backward reading of notes of the original series, starting from the last note of the series and going forward to the first one

Ex. 131

—the **retrograde inversion** [RI] reverses the reading of notes included in the inversion

Ex. 132

As a result of the methods mentioned above, a total of four forms of the series is obtained, any of which can also have eleven transpositions, on all other steps of the chromatic scale.

NOTE: The multiple series—whether tonal, atonal, symmetrical, all interval series, or others—derive from the internal organization of pitch tones.

Ex. 133

—tonal—The intervallic structure suggests a tonal center:

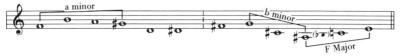

—atonal—There is no tonal attraction between the tones:

—etc.

Ear-Training Exercises

a. Exercise for intonation based on serial technique including all previously mentioned aspects of the row [O, I, R, RI].

NOTE: During the exercise, hold each tone long enough to hear internally the next one to be sung.

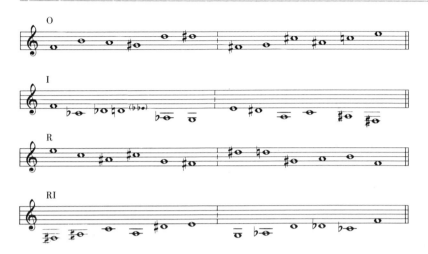

b. Starting from a given note, sing and identify the tones of a short atonal passage, based on non-repetition of tones, played by the instructor.

Ex. 134

Rhythmic Exercises

New rhythmic formula: 𝅗𝅥. = ♩ ♩ ♩

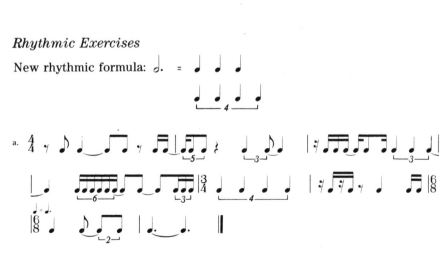

Solfège

170.

Dictation 48

Lesson 49

1. Serial Music (continued)
2. Chords by Seconds

1. The new manner of organizing tones by means of the serial or twelve-tone technique has implications with respect to pitch distribution, rhythm, phrase structure, and dynamics —all of which transform the series into a more "touchable" or understandable thematic organization.

A large variety of manipulations of the series exists:

• One of these techniques is SEGMENTATION, which consists of dividing the series into groups, with each group containing two, three, four, or six tones. The *segments* or *tropes* of the original series can be used in the course of the composition by transforming or combining them with other segments of related series, for the purpose of constructing a complex structure.

• PERMUTATION consists of regrouping the series by every second, third, *etc.* element, thus obtaining new tone-orders.

Ex. 135

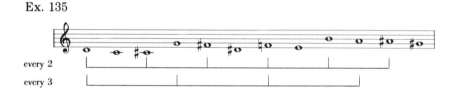

every 2

every 3

• In addition, the serial organization of pitch tones can also extend to other compositional factors such as rhythm, dynamics, and timbre, thus producing INTEGRAL SERIALISM.

—serial organization of *rhythm* involves only the original and retrograde forms with their augmentation and diminution.

Ex. 136

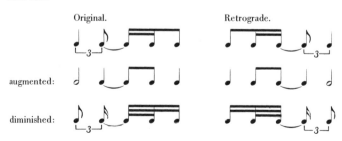

—serial organization can be extended into the areas of **dynamics,** with the possibility of original and retrograde versions.

Ex. 137

Fragment from Solfège 171:

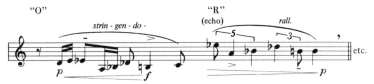

—serial organization of **timbre** also occurs in contemporary music (see the timbre sets of Babbitt's *Composition for Four Instruments*).

2. Besides the other types of chord mentioned previously, twentieth-century music frequently uses CHORDS BY SECONDS which consist of the simultaneous sounding of two or more superimposed Major or minor second intervals.

Ex. 138

Ear-Training Exercises

a. Exercise for intonation based on series organized in three segments, each of which includes four notes.

NOTE: Practice each segment individually and then connect them.

b. Starting from a given note, sing and identify the tones of an atonal segment played by the instructor.

Ex. 139

c. Starting from the following tones, form and sing chords by seconds:

d. Sing and identify the intervals included in the chords below:

e. Identify the chords played by the instructor:

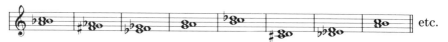

Rhythmic Exercises

New rhythmic development: Exclusion of time-signature.

NOTE: Choose an appropriate tempo, and while performing, tap the regular pulsations, considering the quarter-note-value as the time-unit.

b.

Solfège

Dictation 49

Andantino

Lesson 50

Aleatory Music

In ALEATORY MUSIC the *elements of chance* are introduced in creation, as well as in performance.

Because of the extensive use of this technique by Stockhausen, Boulez, Pousseur, and many others, it is important for any knowledgeable musician to be acquainted with this development and to be able to experiment with the "world of symbols" involved in aleatory music. (See Lesson 51.)

One of the basic features of this process is combinations of determined factors and the elements of chance in a composition. This process may appear in the following aspects:

—aleatorism in terms of *pitch*, involving a choice from many possibilities proposed by the composer, or suggestions for free improvisation of the performer.

Ex. 140

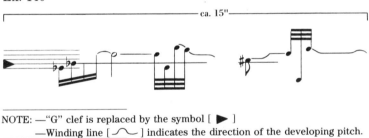

NOTE: —"G" clef is replaced by the symbol [▶]
—Winding line [⌒⌒] indicates the direction of the developing pitch.

—aleatorism of the *duration* of notes may apply to the determined pitch tones. In this process, there are methods to indicate the time in which a certain quantity of tones should be performed. In the example below, this time is marked by seconds ["]. However, within a section, the performance of the note-values depends on the performer.

Ex. 141

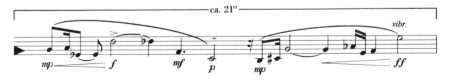

The same example can appear with a more precise graphic denotation that consists of marking the seconds and connecting the notes with lines that approximate how long a note should be held.

Ex. 142

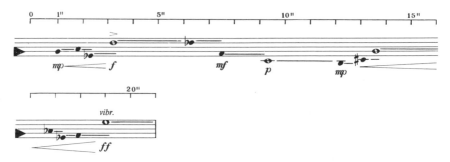

The **structure** of aleatory music can also be **undetermined** because of the multiple possibilities that relations between sounds can acquire. This depends upon the various degrees of freedom of choice given to the performers and also upon the creativity of the performers themselves.

NOTE: **Spatial notation** is one of the frequently used writing techniques of twentieth-century composers, often correlated with aleatorism, by means of substituting spatial representation for traditional notation of the qualities of tone (mainly duration). Because of the versatile and complex nature of this particular writing, definite rules cannot be given here. However, a few examples included in the List of Scores, under the heading "Graphic Symbols and Spatial Notation," present some aspects of this type of notation. For more information, see *Dictionary of Contemporary Music*. John Winton, ed., "Spatial Music."

Ear-Training Exercises

NOTE: The voice, as well as instruments, can be used to perform all the exercises that follow.

a. These exercises are based on pitch improvisation. Each segment should be practiced individually.

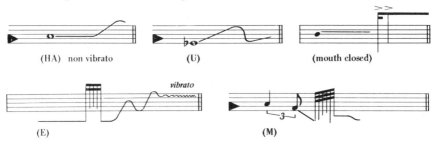

b. Sing the tones of approximate pitch by pronouncing the letters: A, E, M.

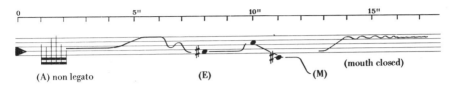

Rhythmic Exercises

New rhythmic development, based on the aleatorism of the duration of notes, will be used in the following exercises:

NOTE:

—The duration of the note-values are indicated by

= long

= short

= very short

—An extension of the beam [♪] of any note-value indicates the approximate duration of the note.

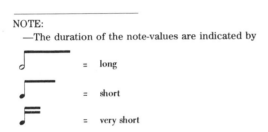

b. Connect the segments below in any order to form a complete exercise:

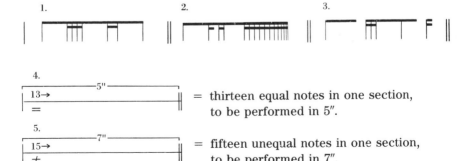

= thirteen equal notes in one section, to be performed in 5".

= fifteen unequal notes in one section, to be performed in 7".

Solfege

NOTE:—Because of the progressive elimination of traditional notation in the last few lessons, the term "solfège" can now be replaced by whatever name the performer chooses to give the exercises below.

—From this point on, directions will be given in the form of a few descriptive comments for performance.

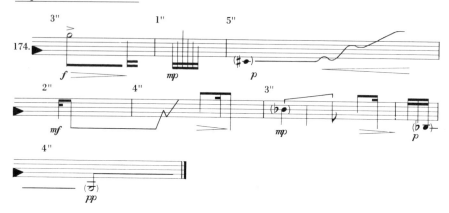

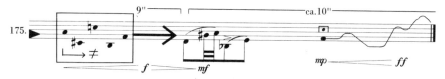

Comment: To be sung.   Silence.   Pitch improvisation.

Nonequal repe-
tition of written
notes in any order
in 9".

According to personal choice, connect the segments below in any order to form the complete exercise.

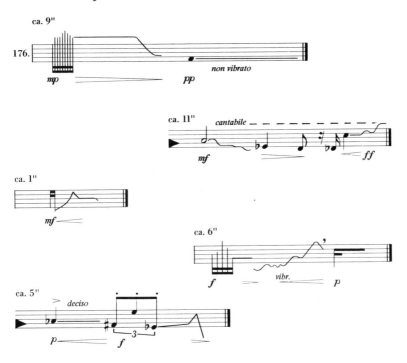

Dictation 50

NOTE: The tones marked by ☐ can be given by the instructor.

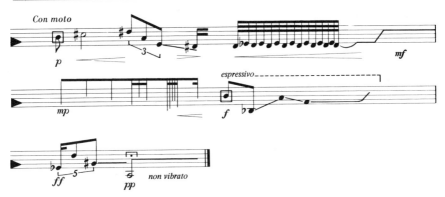

Lesson 51

Aleatory Music: Graphic Symbols

One of the specific features of aleatory music is the extensive use of GRAPHIC SYMBOLS.

Because there is no generally recognized system of notation, the composer usually explains at the beginning of his work, for the sake of clarity, how the symbols are to be performed.

The process of "giving life" to the abstract symbols is a subjective operation that differs from one performer to another. This process generates one of the most interesting aspects of aleatorism, allowing a composition to vary as many times as it is performed.

Graphic symbols can suggest the following qualities:

• appropriate PITCH—high, medium, or low—represented by graphic notation developed vertically with straight or curved lines suggesting the pitch direction.

Ex. 143

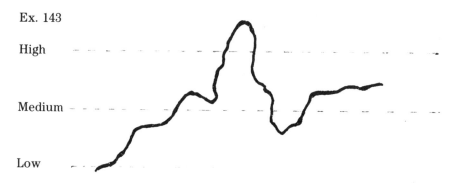

High

Medium

Low

• DURATION—indicated by the space factor of graphic notations developing horizontally to suggest time without actually measuring it.

Ex. 144

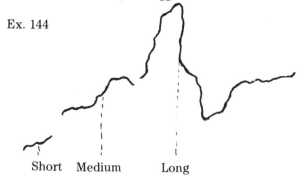

Short   Medium   Long

- INTENSITY or DYNAMICS—suggested by the following procedures:

a. the thickness of a line; the thinner line may indicate a weak intensity while a thicker one symbolizes stronger dynamics.

Ex. 145

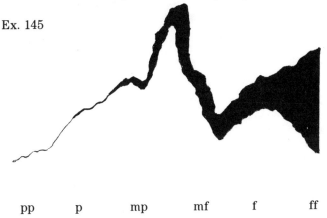

pp	p	mp	mf	f	ff

b. fixed symbols indicated by the composer.

Exp: = crescendo

                            = decrescendo

Ex. 146
(Schäffer: "Azione a due.")

○ ◐ ◑◗ ◑◗ ●◗ ● ●◗
⁻ ppp pp p mp mf f ff fff

NOTE: Often, the meaning of the same symbol differs from one composer to another.

Exp: The symbol ◀━ marks either

1. the intensity = crescendo
2. the tempo = increase of speed

- TIMBRE—has become one of the most important areas for composer experimentation; thus a large number of unusual effects have been introduced:

⊤ = humming

⅄ = tongue click

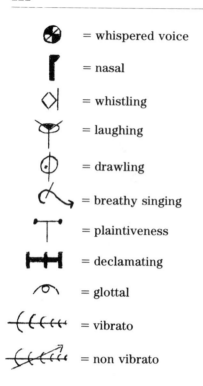

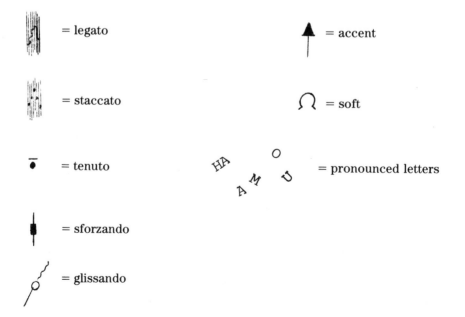

The following graphic symbols are used for articulation:

Other signs:

$\boxed{\bullet}$ = fermata

〰〰 = trill

⎣⎦ = palm clapping

Graphic symbols can also be used to suggest **tempo.**

Ex. 147
(Bussotti: *Il Nudo, Siciliano*)

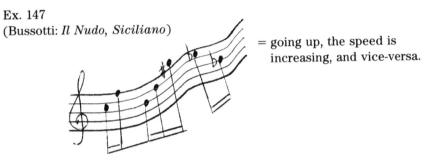

= going up, the speed is
  increasing, and vice-versa.

From E. Karkoschka, *Das Schriftbild der Neuen Musik;* Edited by Moeck Verlag,
Celle, Copyright © 1966 by Moeck Verlag, Celle. Used by permission.

Ex. 148
(Pousseur: *Mobile*)

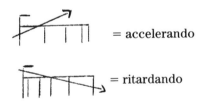

= accelerando

= ritardando

From E. Karkoschka, *Das Schriftbild der Neuen Musik;* Edited by Moeck Verlag,
Celle, Copyright © 1966 by Moeck Verlag, Celle. Used by permission.

NOTE:—Most of the symbols of this lesson have been specially created for the vocal effects
used in the exercises.
    —For more information concerning graphic symbols, see Erhard Karkoschka, *Das
Schriftbild der Neuen Musik;* and John Cage, *Notations.*

Exercises for rhythm and intonation
based on graphic symbols

NOTE:—Each segment should be practiced individually in free tempo.
       —Use any letter to pronounce the tones.

177.
Versions

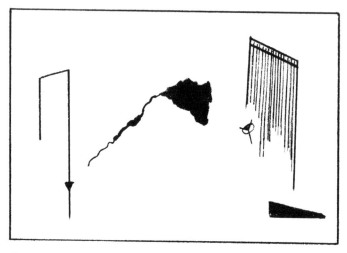

Comment:

Short	Pitch &	Laughing
tones,	rhythm	(decresc.)
the 2nd	improvisation	
is accented		

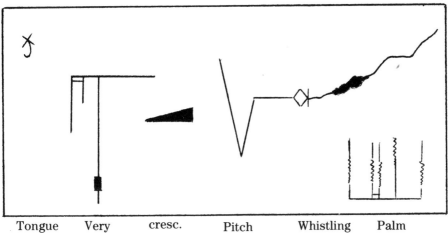

Tongue   Very   cresc.   Pitch   Whistling   Palm
click   short   &   clapping
            tones   rhythm
            (sf.)   improvisation

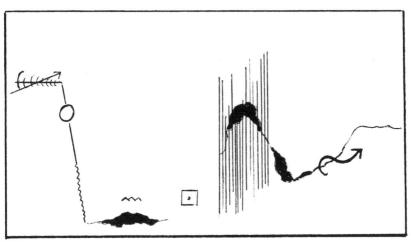

High   Gliss.   Low   Rest   Pitch &   Breathy
tone,   tone   rhythm   singing
non vibrato   (tr.)   improvisation
                                              (legato)

Flux

178.

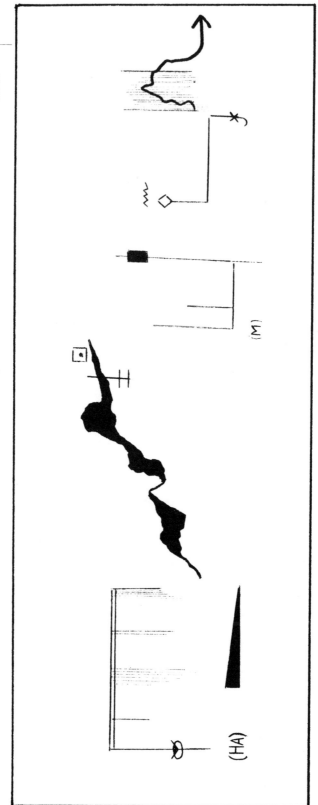

(M)

(HA)

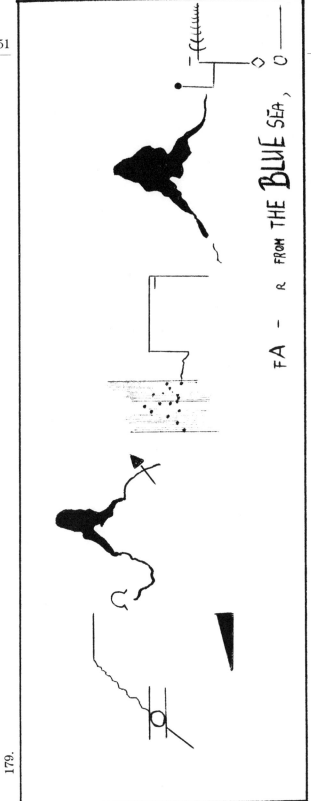

179.

Dictation 51

Shadow

NOTE:—Playing or singing the dictation in the segments below is recommended.

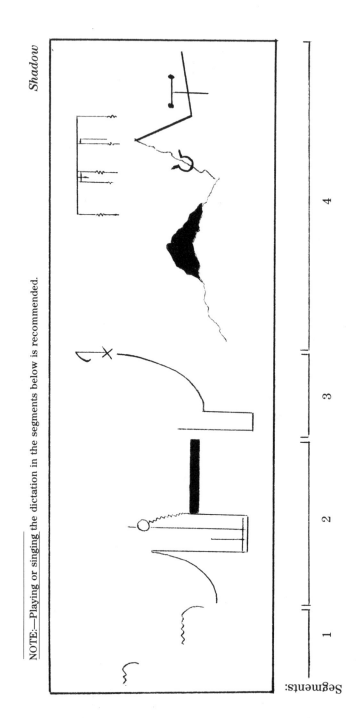

Segments:

1   2   3   4

Musical Examples for Further Reference, illustrating the tonal, chromatic, modal, and atonal systems

Abbreviations used:
Fl. — Flaut
Cor. Ingl. — Corno inglese
Cl. — Clarinet
Fg. — Fagott
Hrs. — Horns

Tr. — Trumpet
Vn. — Violin
Str. Orch. — String Orchestra
Pft. — Piano
Harpsi. — Harpsichord
Fig. Bass — Figured Bass

PART ONE
THE TONAL SYSTEM

* *A. Corelli:*
Concerto Grosso, Op. 6, No. 11, "Sarabanda."

(Vn. concertato)

From Edition Peters No. 4491 by permission of the publisher

* *J. S. Bach:*
The Passion According to S. Matthew, "The sorrows Thou art bearing," Chorale (Part I).

From J. S. Bach, "The sorrows Thou art bearing," Chorale; Edited by G. Schirmer, Inc. New York. Copyright © 1905 by G. Schirmer, Inc. Used by permission.

Brandenburg Concerto No. 1 in F Major (1st Movement).

Concerto for piano No. 2, in d minor (1st Movement).

From Edition Peters No. 4263 by permission of the publisher

Air for the G String, "Gigue."

Reproduced by permission of Ernst Eulenburg Ltd.

French Suite, No. 2, "Courante" Pft.

From J. S. Bach, French Suite, No. 2, in C Minor. Edited by G. Schirmer, Inc., New York. Used by permission.

G. Fr. Handel:
Sonata in g minor, Op. 1, No. 2; Fl. & Continuo

From G. Fr. Handel, Sonata in g minor, Op. 1, No. 2; Edited by Lea Pocket Scores, New York. Used by permission.

Messiah, Oratorio; "Air" Part I, No. 19.

(Soprano)

Re-joice, re-joice, re-joice ____ great-ly,
From G. Fr. Handel, Messiah, Oratorio; Coppersmith Edition. Copyright ©
MCMXLVII by Carl Fischer Inc., New York. All rights reserved. Used by permission.

Concerto Grosso in a minor, Op. 6, No. 4; Str. Orch. (1st Movement).

From Edition Peters No. 4423 by permission of the publisher

D. Scarlatti:
Sonata in D Major, L.465, Harpsi.

From D. Scarlatti, Sonata in D Major, L. 465; Edited by Lea Pocket Scores, New York. Used by permission.

Sonata in E Major, L.430, Harpsi.

* *A. Vivaldi:*
Concerto Grosso in d minor, Op 3, No. 11 (1st Movement).

From Edition Eulenburg Pocket Score No. 750 by permission of the publisher

* *J.Ph. Rameau*
Pièces de Clavecin, Book of 1706, "First Sarabande."

Pièces de Clavecin, Book of 1724, Suite No. 1, "La Villageoise."

From J. Ph. Rameau, Pieces de Clavecin; Edited by Lea Pocket Scores, New York.
Used by permission.

* *Ch. W. Gluck:*
Iphigenia in Aulis, Ouverture (2nd Theme)

From Edition Eulenburg Pocket Score No. 676 by permission of the publisher

* *F. J. Haydn:*
Concerto for trumpet in E Flat Major (1st Movement)

Symphony No. 100, "Military" (4th Movement)

From Edition Eulenburg Pocket Score No. 434 by permission of the publisher

Trio No. 1 in C Major, "London" 2 Fls. & Cello (1st Movement)

From F. J. Haydn, Trio No. 1 in C Major; Edited by Nagels-Verlag, Kassel.
Copyright © 1931 by Adolph Nagel, Hannover. Used by permission.

* W. A. Mozart:

Sonata in F Major, K. 300, Pft. (1st Movement)

From W. A. Mozart, Sonata in F Major; Edited by G. Schirmer, Inc., New York.
Copyright © 1945 by G. Schirmer, Inc. Used by permission.

Concerto for violin in D Major, K. 218 (1st Movement)

From W. A. Mozart, Concerto in D Major for Violin and Orchestra; Edited by
Edwin F. Kalmus, New York. Used by permission.

Requiem, "Tuba mirum" (Basso Solo)

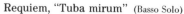

Tu - ba   mirum spargens   so_____   _____num

From Edition Peters No. 76 by permission of the publisher

Deutsche Tänze, No. 3, K.600, Orch.

From W. A. Mozart, Deutsche Tänze No. 3, Edited by Breitkopf & Härtel,
Wiesbaden. Used by permission.

Symphony No. 40, in G Minor, K.550 (3rd Movement)

From Edition Eulenburg Pocket Score No. 404 by permission of the publisher

* L. van Beethoven:

Sonata, Op. 10, No. 3; Pft.

From L. van Beethoven, Sonata Op. 10, No. 3, for Piano; Edited by G. Schirmer,
Inc., New York. Copyright © 1923 by G. Schirmer, Inc., New York. Used by permission.

Serenada, Op. 8. "Minuet"; Vn., Viola & Cello (3rd Movement)

From L. van Beethoven, Serenada Op. 8, for Violin, Viola and Cello. Edited by
Ernst Eulenburg Ltd., London. Used by permission.

String Quartet in F, Op. 59, No. 1 (1st Movement)

(Cello)

From L. van Beethoven, Quartet in F Major, Op. 59, No. 1; Edited by Lea Pocket Scores, New York. Used by permission.

Concerto for piano No. 5, in E Flat Major, Op. 73, "Emperor"; (1st Movement)

From L. van Beethoven, Concerto No. 5, Op. 73, in E Flat Major. Edited by Ernst
Eulenburg Ltd., London. Used by permission.

Symphony No. 6, Op. 68 (5th Movement).

From Edition Eulenburg Pocket Score No. 407 by permission of the publisher

PART TWO
THE CHROMATIC SYSTEM

* N. Paganini:
Caprices, Op. 1, No. 13.

From Edition Peters No. 1984 by permission of the publisher

* H. Berlioz:
Harold in Italy, Op. 16, "Orgy of the Brigands"; Orch. (4th Movement).

From H. Berlioz, Harold in Italy, Op. 16. Edited by Ernst Eulenburg Ltd.,
London. Used by permission.

* Fr. Chopin:
Études, Op. 10, No. 2, in a minor.

From Fr. Chopin, Études, Op. 10, No. 2; Edited by G. Schirmer, Inc., New York.
Copyright © 1916 by G. Schirmer, New York. Used by permission.

* R. Wagner:
Tristan und Isolde, "Isoldens Liebestod."

Mild und   leise   wie   er   lächelt,

wie   das Auge   hold   er - öffnet,   seht ihr's   Freunde?
From Edition Eulenburg Pocket Score No. 649 by permission of the publisher

Tannhäuser, Ouverture.

From Edition Eulenburg Pocket Score No. 669 by permission of the publisher

* J. Brahms:
Symphony No. 3, Op. 90 (3rd Movement).

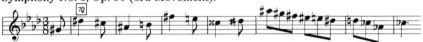

* M. Ravel:
Daphnis et Chloe, Ballet Suite No. 1, Orch. (3rd Movement).

* P. Dukas:
L'Apprenti sorcier, Scherzo.

* R. Korsakov:
Scheherazade, Op. 35; Orch. (1st Movement).

* G. Mahler:
Symphony No. 4 (3rd Movement).

* S. Prokofieff:
Symphony No. 6, Op. 111 (1st Movement)

* D. Shostakovich:

Symphony No. 7, Op. 60 (1st Movement).

* I. Stravinsky:

The Rite of Spring, "Dance of the Adolescents," Orch.

The Fire Bird, Ballet Suite, Part I, Orch.

* A. Scriabin:

"Le Poème de l'extase", Symphonic Poem, Op. 34.

PART THREE
THE MODAL SYSTEM

SECTION A: Pentatonic Scales (Modes)

* Fuki No Kyoku (Japanese accompanied Song);

* *Komori-Uta* ("Cradle Song," Japanese Folk Song, transcribed by Kosçak Yamada).

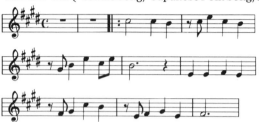

* *Hua Ku Ko-Noi* ("The Flower Drum," Chinese Folk Song, transcribed by Chin-Hsin Yao Chen and Shih-Hsiang Chen).

* *Felszállott a páva* (Hungarian folk song, transcribed by Pál Járdányi).

* *Cununa* (Romanian folk song, transcribed by Il. Ćocişiu).

SECTION B: Medieval Modes

IONIAN:

Sumer is icumen in (c. 1310).

* *Guillaume Dufay* (c. 1400-1474), "Alma redemptoris mater," Antiphon B.M.V.

Al -   ma   redemptoris ma - ter,

DORIAN:

* *School of Notre Dame* (c. 1200), "Domino" (Clausula).

(Chorus)

De - o gra -   ti - as.

* *Troubadour Song* (12th cent., from original manuscript at St. Martial in Limoges).

* *Girolamo Cavazzoni* (b.c. 1515), "Missa Apostolorum" (Cunctipotens) Organ
Mass, Kyrie primus.

Ky - ri - e   e -   le - i - son.

PHRYGIAN

* *Leonhard Kleber* (1524), Tablature, Preambulum in "mi."

* Huic main - Hec dies Motet (13th c.).

LYDIAN:

* Neithart von Reuenthal (d.c. 1240) "Der May."

* Hymn from the Octoechos, Byzantine Chant (13th cent.)

MIXOLYDIAN:

* Christo psallat, Rondellus (Early Medieval Music)

* *School of Worcester* (14th cent.) "Alleluia psallat," Motet.

AEOLIAN:

* *St. Godric* (d. 1170), "Sainte Marie," English song.

* *Richard Coeur-de-Lion* (1157–1199) "Ja nuns hons pris," Ballade.

LOCRIAN:

* *"Colindă"* from Muntenia, Romania.

SECTION C: Modern and Contemporary Modes

WHOLE-TONE writing:

* *Cl. Debussy:*
Prélude a L'Après-midi d'un faune, Orch.

La Mer, "Jeux de vagues," Orch. (2nd Movement).

* *Bela Bartók:*
The Wonderful Mandarin, Op. 19, Orch.

I. Stravinsky:
Petrouchka, Suite Ballet, Tableau 3, "Chez la Maure" Orch.
(I Vn.)

THE MODES of O. MESSIAEN:

Turangalîla — Symphonie, Introduction (uses all the notes of Mode 1).
(Pft.)

Visions de l'Amen pour deux pianos, "Amen de l'agonie de Jésus", Part III (uses all
the notes of Mode 2).
(2nd piano)

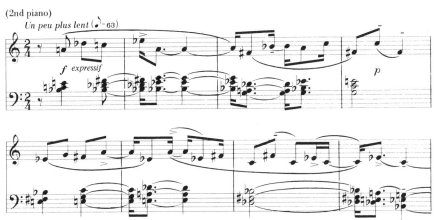

Thème et variations, pour violin & piano, 4th Variation (uses all the notes of Mode 3).

Turangalîla — Symphonie Part VIII "Developpement de l'amour" (uses partially the notes of Mode 4).

Préludes, "Les sons impalpables du rêve"; Pft. (uses all the notes of Mode 6).

Vingt Regards sur l'Enfant Jésus, Part X, "Regard de l'Esprit de joie", Pft. (uses partially the notes of Mode 7).

PART FOUR
THE ATONAL SYSTEM

"FREE" ATONAL writing:

* A. Schönberg:
Erwartung, Op. 17.

From A. Schönberg, Erwartung, Op. 17; Edited by Universal Edition, A. G., Wien.
Copyright © 1922 by Universal Edition A. G., Wien. Used by permission.

Pierrot Lunaire, Op. 21, I Teil, "Mondestrunken."

* A. Webern:
Six Pieces, Op. 6, Orch. (6th Movement).

6 Bagatellen für Streichquartett (1st Movement).

From A. Webern, 6 Bagatellen für Streichquartett; Edited by Universal Edition.
Copyright © 1924 by Universal Edition A. G., Wien. Used by permission.

TWELVE-TONE (SERIAL) writing:

A. Schönberg:
Variations for Orchestra, Op. 31.

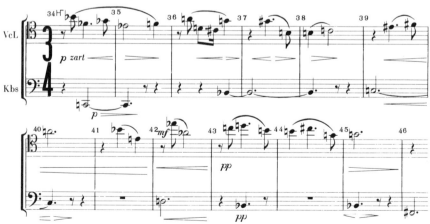

From A. Schönberg, Variations for Orchestra, Op. 31; Edited by Universal
Edition. Copyright © 1929 by Universal Edition A. G., Wien. Used by permission.

Phantasy, for Violin with Piano Accomp. Op. 47.

Klavierstück, Op. 33a.

A. Webern:
Symphonie Op. 21 (1st Movement).

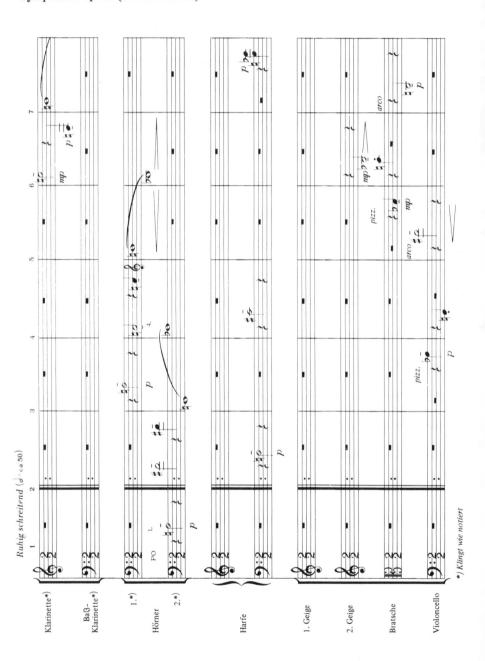

From A. Webern, Symphonie, Op. 21; Edited by Universal Edition. Copyright ©
1929 by Universal Edition A. G., Wien. Used by permission.

(2nd Movement, "Variationen").

From A Webern, Symphonie, Op. 21; Edited by Universal Edition. Copyright ©
1929 by Universal Edition A. G., Wien. Used by permission.

String Trio, Op. 20 (1st Movement).

From A. Webern, String Trio, Op. 20; Edited by Universal Edition. Copyright ©
1927 by Universal Edition A. G., Wien. Used by permission.

A. Berg:
Lyric Suite, String Quartet (1st Movement).

From A. Berg, Lyric Suite; Edited by Universal Edition. Copyright © 1927 by
Universal Edition A. G., Wien. USED BY PERMISSION.

P. Boulez:
Le Soleil des eaux, "Complainte du Lezard Amoreaux"; Orch.

Avec l'autorisation des Editions Heugel et Cie. — Paris.

GRAPHIC SYMBOLS and SPATIAL NOTATION:

* *G. Crumb:*
Night Music I (6th Movement).

senza misura; improvvisato
5

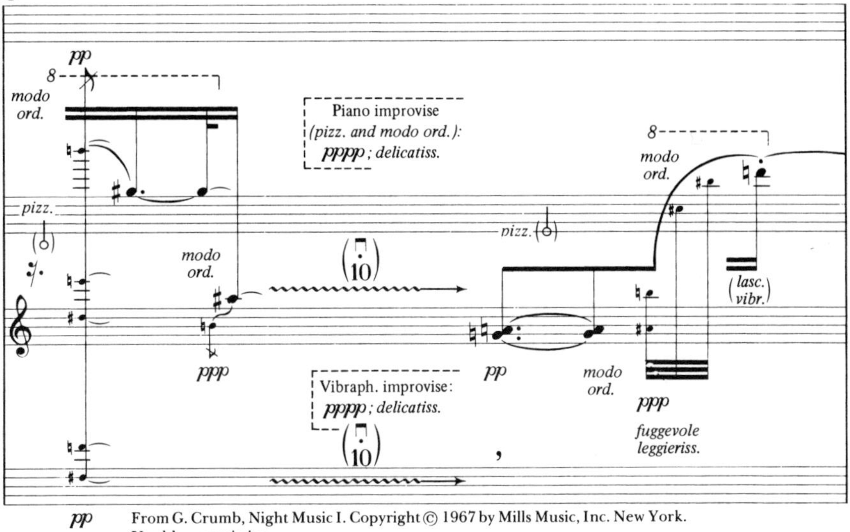

* *H. Haubenstock-Ramati:*
Symphonie 'K.'

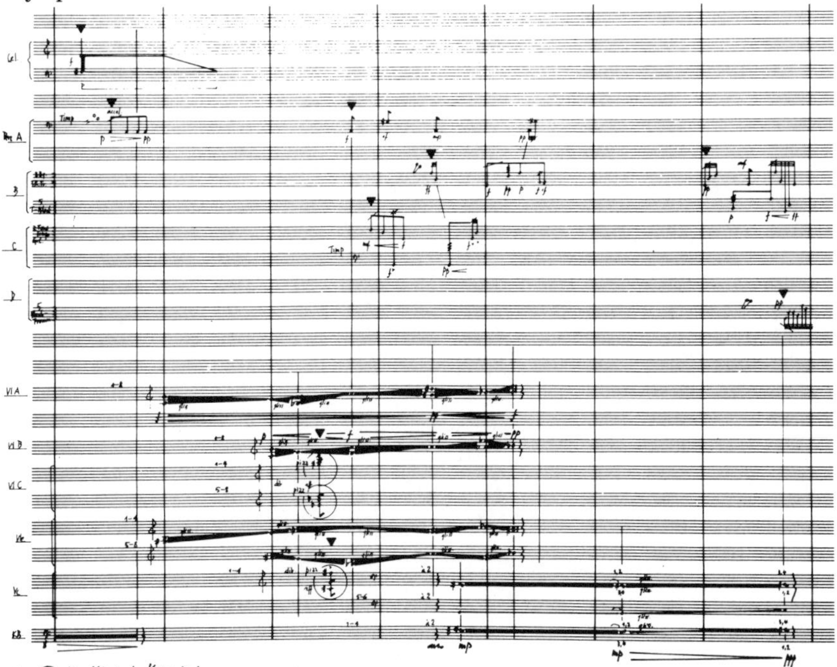

* W. Lutosławsky:
Three Poems by Henry Michaux, "Pensées."

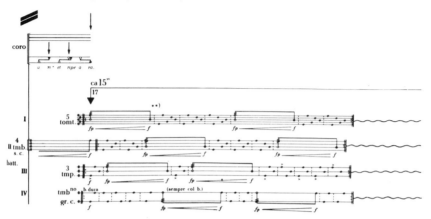

* L. Berio:
Circles

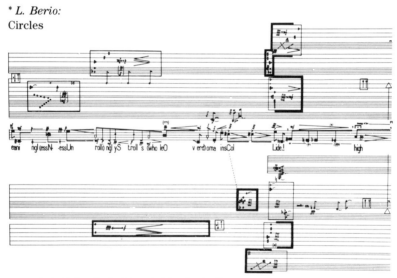

* M. Powell:
Filigree Settings, for String Quartet.

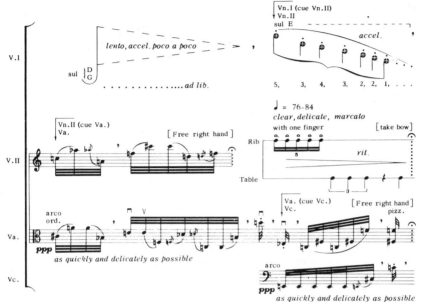

From M. Powell, Filigree Setting; Edited by G. Schirmer, Inc. Copyright ©
MCMLXV by G. Schirmer, Inc., New York. Used by permission.

* B. Schäffer:
Scultura

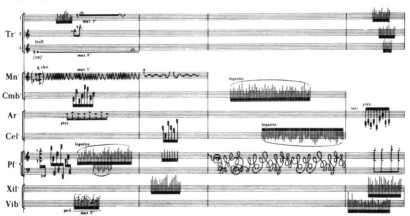

From B. Schäffer, Scultura, edited by PWM-Edition Krakow Poland. Copyright ©
1967 by PWP-Warsaw Poland. Used by permission.

S. Bussotti:

Fragmentations pour un joeur de Harpes.

From S. Bussotti, Fragmentations pour un joeur de Harpes; Edited by Aldo
Bruzzichelli. Copyright © 1963 by Aldo Bruzzichelli. Used by permission.

K. Penderecki:

Dies Irae, oratorium ob memoriam in perniciei castris in Oswiecim necatorum
inextinguibilem reddendam. Copyright © 1967 by Polskie Wydawnictwo Muzyczne, Kraków, Poland, for all
Socialist Countries of the world. Copyright © 1967 by Moeck Verlag, Celle, for
the rest of the world. Used by permission.

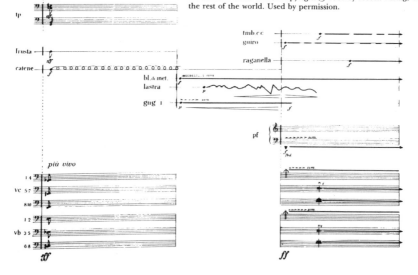

D. Ghezzo:
Thalla, Music for piano and 16 instruments.

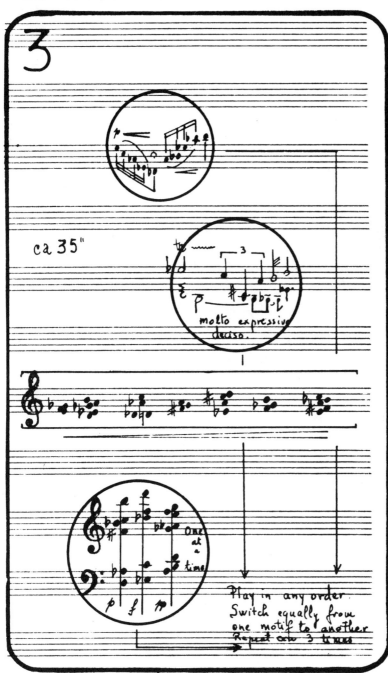

From "THALLA," Music for Pianos and 16 Instruments by DINU GHEZZO.
Copyright © 1975 by Seesaw Music Corp., New York. Used by permission.

P. Renosto:
Avant d'Écrire (Part 5).

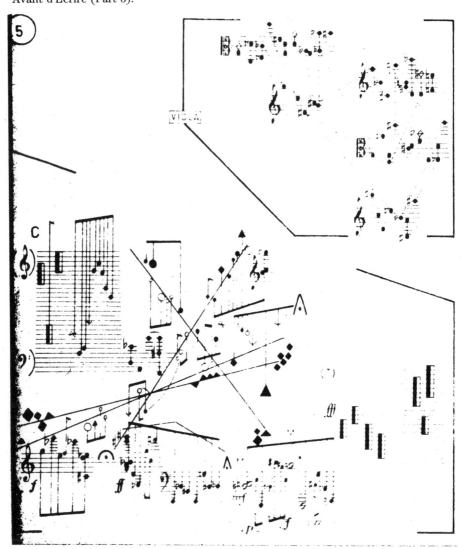

K. Stockhausen:
Nr. 12 Kontakte.

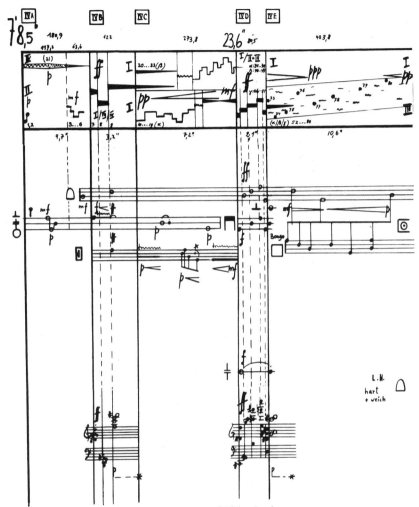

From K. Stockhausen, Nr. 12 Kontakte; Edited by Universal Edition, London.
Copyright © 1966 by Universal Edition (London) Ltd., London. Used by
permission.

R. Reynolds:
Traces (Part 'H').

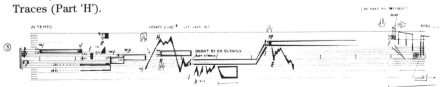

From Edition Peters No. 66247. Copyright © 1969 by C. F. Peters Corporation,
373 Park Avenue South, New York, N.Y. 10016. Reprint permission granted by
the publisher.

J. Cage:
Aria.

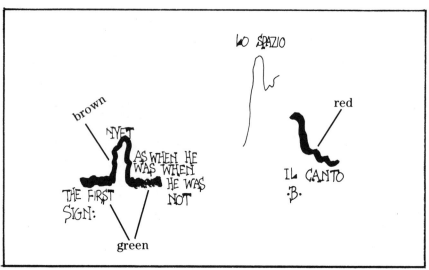

The color indications of the above fragment are given by the author.

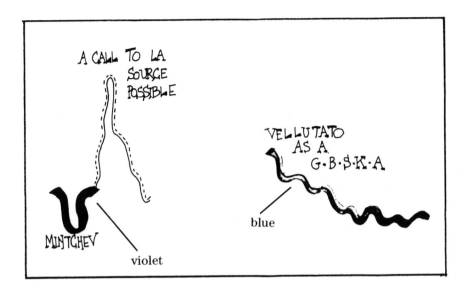

* *Gy. Ligeti:*
Volumina (1961).

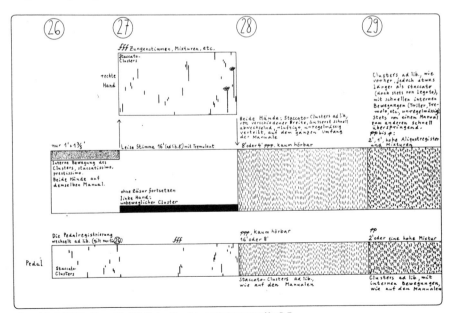

Bibliography

Books

Apel, Willi. *Harvard Dictionary of Music.* Cambridge: Harvard University Press, 1944; 2nd revised edition, 1969.

Bacon, Richard Mackenzie. *Elements of Vocal Science, being a Philosophical Enquiry into Some of the Principles of Singing.* Pro Musica Press, 1966.

Bukofzer, Manfred F. *Music in the Baroque Era.* New York: W. W. Norton & Co., Inc., 1947.

Cage, John. *Silence, lectures and writings.* Middletown: Wesleyan University Press, 1961.

Collaer, Paul. *A History of Modern Music.* New York: The Universal Library, Grosset & Dunlap, 1961.

Comisel, Emilia. *Folclor Musical.* Bucharest: Editura Didactică si Pedagogică, 1967.

Crocker, Richard L. *A History of Musical Style.* New York: McGraw-Hill, 1966.

Cross, Milton and David Ewen. *The Milton Cross New Encyclopedia of the Great Composers and Their Music.* 2 vols. New York, Garden City: Doubleday & Company, Inc., 1969.

Ffrangcon, D.-Davies, *The Singing of the Future.* New York: John Lane Co., 1905.

Foreman, Edward. *The Porpora Tradition.* Pro Musica Press, 1968.

Garcia, Manuel. *Hints on Singing.* Summit Publishing Co., 1970

Giuleanu, V. and V. Iusceanu, *Tratat de Teorie a Muzicii.* Bucharest: Editura Muzicală a Uniunii Compositorilor din R.P.R., 1962.

Grout, D. J. *A History of Western Music.* New York: W. W. Norton & Co., 1960.

Henderson, W. J. *The Art of Singing.* New York: The Dial Press, 1938.

Karkoschka, Erhard. *Das Schriftbild der Neuen Music.* Celle: Herman Moeck Verlag, 1966.

Lang, Paul Henry and Nathan Broder. *Contemporary Music in Europe: A Comprehensive Survey.* The Norton Library, W. W. Norton and Co., Inc., 1968

Messiaen, Olivier. *Technique de mon langage musical,* 2 vols. Paris: Alphonse Leduc et Cie, Édition Musicales, 1956.

Myer, Edmund J. *The Renaissance of the Vocal Art.* Boston: The Boston Music Co., 1902.

Olson, Harry F. *Music, Physics* and *Engineering.* New York: Dover Publications, Inc., 1967.

Parisot, Dom J. *Rapport sur une mission scientifique en Turque D'Asie.* Paris: Imprimerie Nationale, Ernes Leroux, 1897.

Parrish, Carl. *A Treasury of Early Music.* New York: W. W. Norton & Co., Inc., 1958.

Perle, George. *Serial Composition and Atonality.* University of California Press, 1968.

Persichetti, Vincent. *Twentieth Century Harmony.* New York: W. W. Norton & Co., 1961.

Reese, Gustave. *Music in the Renaissance.* New York: W. W. Norton & Co., 1959.

Salzman, Eric. *Twentieth Century Music: An Introduction.* New Jersey: Prentice-Hall, Inc., 1967.

Schiøtz, Aksel. *The Singer and His Art.* New York: Harper & Row Publishers, 1970.

Seay, Albert. *Music in the Medieval World.* Englewood Cliffs, New Jersey: Prentice-Hall, 1965.

Smith, Brindle Reginald. *Serial Composition and Atonality.* University of California Press, 1968.

Stuckenschmidt, H. H. *Twentieth Century Music.* World University Library, 1969.

Ulrich, Homer and Paul A. Pisk. *A History of Music and Musical Style.* New York: Harcourt, Brace & World, Inc., 1963.